CATCHING FIRE

CATCHING FIRE

THE LOS ANGELES WILDFIRES JANUARY 5– FEBRUARY 1, 2025

EDITED BY

S.A. GRIFFIN & RICHARD MODIANO

Rose Of Sharon
PRESS
LOS ANGELES

Catching Fire: The Los Angeles Wildefires: January 5–February 1, 2025
EDITED BY S.A. Griffin and Richard Modiano

© Copyright 2026 by Rose of Sharon Press | An imprint of Three Rooms Press

All rights reserved. No part of this book may be reproduced in any form or by any electronic or mechanical means, including information storage and retrieval systems, without permission in writing from the publisher, except by a reviewer, who may quote brief passages in a review. Please direct all inquiries to carmabum@gmail.com. Any members of educational institutions wishing to photocopy or electronically reproduce part or all of the work for classroom use, or publishers who would like to obtain permission to include the work in an anthology, should email their inquiries to Rose of Sharon Press via carmabum@gmail.com.

ISBN 978-1-513677-71-2 (trade paper original)

Publication Date: January 5, 2026 | First edition

ACKNOWLEDGEMENTS:
"The Eaton Fire, Altadena, CA, January 7-8, 2025" by Mary Anne Berry first appeared in *Altadena Poetry Review – Virtual Edition*, 2024–25.
"Fire Roulette" by Jeanette Clough first appeared in *Fire Roulette* (Cahuenga Press, 2025).
"Oxygen" by Brendan Constantine first appeared in *The Baltimore Review* (2023), and *The Opposites Game* from Red Hen Press in March 2026.
"Strange Grace" by Phoebe MacAdams first published in *Strange Grace* (Cahuenga Press, 2007).
"Something Thrown Away" by Sarah Maclay first appeared in *Whore: Poems* (U of Tampa Press, 2004).
"Wild Fire" by Majid Naficy first appeared in both English and Persian on his blog *Iroon.com* after the Sand Fire in Los Angeles County, 2016.
"listening to your playlist while driving made me feel like i was in your car again going around l.a." by jimmy vega first appeared in *Westwind: UCLA's Journal of the Arts* Spring Journal 2023.

BISAC Coding:
POE023010 POETRY / Subjects & Themes / Death, Grief, Loss
POE004010 POETRY / American / General
POE001000 POETRY / Anthologies (multiple authors)
LCO002000 LITERARY COLLECTIONS / American / General

COVER:
Cover photo of Michelle Bitting's PhD mortar boards and vintage typewriter (1957 Royal Quiet De Luxe), photo by Phil Abrams.

BOOK DESIGN:
KG Design International: www.katgeorges.com

DISTRIBUTED IN THE U.S. AND INTERNATIONALLY BY:
Publishers Group West: www.pgw.com

Rose of Sharon Press | Los Angeles, CA, an imprint of
Three Rooms Press | New York, NY | www.threeroomspress.com

Dedicated to the courageous firefighters from Los Angeles County and beyond. These women and men are true heroes.

We are Lost Angeles.
We rise.

Table of Contents (First lines and titles)

Introduction – S.A. Griffin..i
There is no hope – Z...1
Hurricane of Fire – Dig Wayne 2
In the Shadow of the Unicorn – Puma Perl.........................3
Dateline Altadena, California – Suan Auerbach.....................4
What Was Waiting at the Front Door – Kathleen Florence 6
Perello Family's Journey to Re-Establish Our Lives
    (January 2025) – Cynthia Perello............................7
And This Too Shall Burn... – A.K. Toney 9
Catastrophe... – Dan Saucedo 11
The Ojai Fire – Phoebe MacAdams.................................12
A Sense of Urgency – Cathie Sandstrom...........................14
Non-Sonnet for Burning – Iris De Anda...........................15
Fire Ecology – Mike Sonksen 16
Ice and Fire – David L. Ulin.....................................17
ghost town – Nicca Ray..19
My Sadness is as Great as a Mountain: A Haibun – Teresa Mei Chuc 21
Perello Family's Journey to Re-Establish Our Lives
    (February 23, 2025) – Cynthia Perello.......................23
Water Hose Man – Pam Ward 24
Ashes Over Angels – Richard Modiano 26
Fire Head – Rich Ferguson 27
Sudden – Michelle Bitting 30
What Remains – Ellyn Maybe 32
Walking Home on 14th Street – Hilda Weiss 33
L.A. Fires and Me – Marilyn N. Robertson 35
The Eaton Fire, Altadena, CA, January 7-8, 2025 –
    Mary Anne Berry 36
Mother Nature Talks Back – Laurel Ann Bogen 38
Oxygen – Brendan Constantine....................................39
A Drive Along the Coast – Harry Northup 40
A History of Fire Drills – Susan Hayden 41
Equal Footing – Kat Georges.....................................45
Winds-Day - Spencer L. Griffin 47
Snow Born From Flames – Riot Renwick.......................... 48
It Seemed the Sea was Speaking in Tongues – Suzanne Lummis 49

Canyon Country – Tom Laichas..51
Wild Fire – Majid Naficy 53
What I Didn't Lose in the Great L.A. Fires – Maryrose Smyth 55
4 Haiku – Land Flowers 63
Fire Roulette – Jeanette Clough 65
Perello Family's Journey to Re-Establish Our Lives
    (March 17, 2025) – Cynthia Perello 65
A New Plague – Rick Lupert 67
Something Thrown Away – Sarah Maclay 69
Shockproof – Chris Morris 71
Singed Memories – Jessica M. Wilson 73
If all my dreams had come true... – Kamla Maya 75
State Farm Said to Keep a Journal but
    I Wrote a Poem Instead – Lin Nelson Benedek 76
Perello Family's Journey to Re-Establish Our Lives
    (July 1, 2025) – Cynthia Perello 83
And Then the Fires Came – Kennon B. Raines 84
Like a Movie – Jim Natal... 88
Wild winds whipped war... – Mona Jean Cedar 90
To the Living, Breathing Arsonists,
    the Molochs of Electricity – Bill Mohr 91
Rivers of Debris Quilt the Sand at Low Tide –
    Holaday Mason 92
The Arsonist – Jeffrey Bryant 93
And for California, it's Only June – Beth Ruscio 94
Wildfires, Redux. – Alexis Rhone Fancher............................95
Ashes at Random – jerry the priest 96
Antidote for a Firestorm – Lynne Bronstein 98
I Know Too Well – Gail Wronsky.....................................100
listening to your playlist while driving made me feel like
    i was in your car again going around l.a. – jimmy vega..........102
The Renter Key – Steve Hochman 104
Pagamento – K.R. Morrison 108
Perello Family's Journey to Re-Establish Our Lives
    (July 25, 2025) – Cynthia Perello 111
WE WILL REBUILD – La Rombé ♪ 113

ABOUT THE CONTRIBUTORS..115

INTRODUCTION

Fueled by dry conditions and relentless Santa Ana winds rushing over the landscape with speeds upwards of 100 mile per hour, everything bending to the will of the wind, the spark of the January fires exploded into an unprecedented gut-wrenching apocalypse. Southern Californians watched 24/7 on the local news waiting for the blaze to reach their homes and businesses as the soul crushing fires mercilessly flooded entire neighborhoods, swallowing much of Altadena (Eaton Fire), the Pacific Palisades (Palisades Fire) and great swaths of Malibu's California coastline along historic Highway 1, leaving behind smoldering ash and rubble in the epic wake taking with it much of the native flora and fauna, devastating much of the affected ecosystems. Generations of unique culture and history that can never be replaced were gone in seconds as we silently watched dreams and memories go up in smoke.

The loss of 31 human lives is attributed to the fires. However, according to a report from the *Journal of American Medicine* published August 7, 2025, the fires contributed to at least 440 deaths during this period, making the fires one of the worst natural disasters in California's history. According to a report from the UCLA Anderson School of Management, over 16,000 structures including homes and businesses were destroyed: 6,837 in Pacific Palisades and Malibu and 9,414 structures in Altadena and Pasadena. The total property and capital losses are estimated between $95 and $164 billion dollars. As reported by CNN and *The New York Times*, the Pasadena Humane Society took in at least 610 animals including dogs, cats, pigs and a pony. Many less fortunate animals and beloved family pets were displaced or very likely perished. Precise figures remain unavailable.

From day one we began getting constant phone calls, texts and emails. Concerned friends and family from across the globe worried that we may have lost everything as a parade of hellish images streamed into their living rooms. And from day one, we began receiving tragic reports from friends and extended family of evacuations and unimaginable losses.

My ex-wife Sharon, our son Spencer and their cat Clarence, who live in Pasadena off Lake Avenue, were evacuated that first night, spending the entire week with my wife Lorraine and I at our apartment in Silver Lake. Cats can be very territorial with space and jealously possessive of their humans. Thankfully, our old cat Rosy fell in with the situation accepting Clarence without hesitation. It was a relief to have them safely here.

On Thursday of that week, fire broke out in Hollywood close to the corner of Hollywood and Franklin in the vicinity of Mann's Chinese Theatre. Receiving a standby alert on our iPhones to evacuate, we immediately began to pack up what we could as we tried to keep a lid on our already tightly wound anxieties. As we packed, we saw images on the local news of frantic drivers at a standstill, a bumper-to-bumper parking lot jamming all possible escape routes leading out of the area like a scene out of the classic sci-fi film *War of the Worlds*. We began openly debating about what might be the safest, smartest and best way around the tangled traffic, worried that we might be caught by the raging inferno, trapped in our car while attempting to escape. We made phone calls to friends much further south to see if they could take us in, cats and all. Then came the alert taking us off standby, time to evacuate.

Just as we were about to beat feet out the door, the alert was called off.

Due to the tremendous bravery of the firefighters and the Santa Ana winds finally ebbing to an acceptable 25 miles per hour allowing the water bearing helicopters to come in and douse the erupting blaze before it moved much further east, we were saved. I cannot say enough about the incredible heroism of all the firefighters from Los Angeles County and beyond.

Their extraordinary courage and fortitude are superhuman. Our praise and gratitude for them is immeasurable.

A few days post apocalypse, I received a call from my longtime poet friend Kat Georges, a native of Orange County just south of here. Kat, along with her partner and husband Peter Carlaftes, are the publisher/editors of Three Rooms Press in New York City. Kat was checking in to see how we were holding up. As we talked, she told me that our mutual friend Puma Perl, a native New Yorker, had relayed to her that another mutual friend, Los Angeles native Nicca Ray, a New York transplant, had been devastated, helplessly watching from across the continent as her hometown of Los Angeles and the surrounding cities burned, succumbing to the fever and fury of the insatiable fire.

After I put down the phone, the bells rang.

This book is the result.

My sincerest thanks to everyone in this anthology for contributing their work. My thanks to Kat and Peter at Three Rooms Press for their help in completing this book, Sarah Maclay who championed the book from the beginning, my Beat brother Richard Modiano for his editorial assist, my wonderful wife Lorraine for her never ending love and support, and to Nicca Ray for the loving spark that ignited *Catching Fire*. Lastly, I'd like to thank Dr. Scott Cherkasky, who keeps the lights on in dark rooms so that I might find my way out from time to time. For like Virgil, he too sees through windows of the soul.

We are Los Angeles.

S.A. Griffin
Publisher, editor Rose of Sharon Press
August 19, 2025

CATCHING FIRE

There is no hope in heaven,
In hell there is nothing but hope.

- Z

Hurricane of Fire

we never learned in school that we are paper;
our bodies delicate strips of humanity
we can we cry until we are soaked
through and through with sorrow
flimsy to the touch like spit balls on the moon
we prepare ourselves for the unknown by
believing everything will be alright
we will be saved
we are good
we are resilient
we will bounce back
there are silos full of gratefulness
gratitude
hope
when we ignore the inconvenience of inconvenience
reality has a way of tipping the balance as a reminder
of how little we understand of what exactly we are made
pulp
grizzle
ash
fear
luck
love
the sweet smell of sweaty children
all grown up
running toward the future
with the deafening sound of
tens of thousands of hearts
breaking all at once

– Dig Wayne

In the Shadow of the Unicorn

Some days there is no poem.
There are no unicorns either.

Just our hearts beating in Los Angeles
wishing it all away,
helpless helpless helpless
like a Neil Young song.

Do we continue to survive and forget
and then it happens again, and we survive
we forget, we survive, some of us,
and we try to forget but we're helpless.

The unicorns have fallen into the wind,
lying on their sides like the sad little
Christmas trees on my Lower East Side block,
blue and red ornaments wrapped up in tinsel
rolling through the frozen streets.

In the shadow of the unicorn
we wait and pray and sing sad songs.

It is much too early for a poem
barely an extra moment to gaze
out the window at our woe begotten streets.

– **Puma Perl**

Dateline Altadena, California
January, 2025

Overnight, my hometown
blazes apocalyptic
on phones around the world.
I cannot follow how
the tyrant floods the zone
but I must read every update
on this fire: the dead
(blessedly few),
the containment (so slow
to reach 5%),
the heroes (or madmen)
who stayed behind wielding hoses.
Each day on the county damage map,
little red houses mushroom
like Monopoly pieces
on a winning board except
we are losing: 6,000 buildings,
8,000, 9,000, more.

    I drive by flattened streets, all rubble and ash—
        I think of Rafah, Mariupol.
    I'm displaced for weeks, others for months—
        How the years drag on for refugees.
    So many neighbors suddenly homeless—
        Will some wander the city with shopping carts?

This is our nuclear winter,
our climate-crisis Pompeii.

A hawk and a helicopter
circle the burn zone, hunting.

We all live inside the news now.

– Susan Auerbach

What Was Waiting at the Front Door

Bags stuffed with papers, passports, tax returns,
medications, laptops, iPad, chargers tangled up.

That jacket I only wore once, I swear, I'll wear it
again, some night when hell isn't hovering

blocks away, just north of here in what will be
known as the Sunset fire.

North, in both directions, panic-painted
nightmares hang in every room.

No one is sleeping, every hour checking screens,
making calls, scanning from rooftops,

beneath bone-shattered skies with each other,
and these few bags at the door, waiting.

– Kathleen Florence

Perello Family's Journey to Re-Establish Our Lives
Go Fund Me, January 2025

Hello friends and family.

We are Ibarionex and Cynthia Perello of Altadena, California and we are seeking support to get back on our feet.

As you can imagine, the horror we and so many others experienced as a result of the destruction the Eaton fires caused in our little (but mighty) city of Altadena, CA, a horrible devastation, to say the least.

Our spirits are torn, we are heartbroken beyond measure, and yet we're still trying to pull ourselves up by the bootstraps in the midst of this situation to re-establish our lives, as well as support others in need.

January 8th, we lost EVERYTHING in this fire.

Evacuating: Initially, when we saw the flames of fire glowing nearby, it was a familiar scene.

The high-velocity winds that propelled the fire had a physical voice—an angry and unforgiving one—and it blew glowing embers and smoke in our direction. With no power, no light, and no reliable means of emergency information. We knew we had to leave our beloved home quickly.

There was an electrical outage that night, so we used the flashlights from our smartphones to retrieve a few essential items, including medications, electronics, a hard drive, and a large bag of dog food. The cremations of my sister-in-law Jacquelyn and the urns/ashes from our furbabies, Traci, Spencer and most recently, Zoey our beloved spirit-pup. We fumbled around a darkened house, trying to remain calm and yet think reasonably while faced with an impossible situation.

We had minutes to evacuate our beloved home. We literally left with the shirts on our backs, pajama pants, the slippers we were wearing, along with our recently adopted furbaby, Gracie.

As most of you know, we lost my beloved mom in 2022, and we made sure to take framed photos of her and family members, etc.

We tried to take what we could and reluctantly left everything of any monetary or sentimental value behind. My tears are flowing heavily as I continue to bravely type these words.

We are grateful to be alive; however, we are sad that some were not able to say the same.

Everything is gone.

We'll never hear or see those familiar sights, scents, or sounds of comfort, which made our home a place of love and comfort that Ibarionex and I spent years building a life together, along with those we've always opened our house up to.

For those who mourn on various levels of loss, we share your deep pain. You are not alone. We are with you and support you 100%.

We are praying for all those affected by these fires, for our neighbors and friends who also experienced loss, and for our beautiful Altadena.

Every contribution, no matter how small or large, will make a significant difference in our recovery journey.

Our family graciously welcomes any donations.

– **Cynthia Perello (Team Perello)**

And This Too Shall Burn . . .

We are all wounds inflamed with remembrance...
It haunts like the present is with us, but as the past burns away
Your normal is no longer a precious future your way
Tell us Prometheus how does one burn sound to a cinder?
Explain plane equipment tools melting or smelting
Like Icarus flying too high in California sunshine
Dreams as wax dripping feathers floating while stripping

Explain how many of Jazz Messenger Drummer's
Toms, snares, bass, cymbals, the kits, mics, recording
    equipment, MPC 3000, interfaces
And the house is a given . . . Nevermind the green tree and
    garden giving in the backyard
How did that become a metaphor for a steel drum barrel with
    fire burning inside?

Give us reason for Daddy Kev's mastering of sound
Becoming unfound to a profound loss in flames . . .
How it still lives on in the clouds if ever such . . .
Analogue equipment, tape recordings, digital equipment, 808,
    SP 1200, SP 404, recording boards
Grammy certificates, musical award precious metal records
    scorched
Valued vinyl in hot waves rolling like cannolis instead of
    spinning to be heard
And the house is a given . . . the private studio for listening
Purpose and work . . .
How does music sound when it incinerates?

What does a mushroom bloom explosion sound like to
    Kevin Sandbloom
When guitar and bass strings ping curl then shrink from
Heat and sound amplifiers cave into ash after embering
The last of ivory and ebony stretching as piano chords popping
And the house is a given . . . the old wooden sound shack
Which was a garage now instantly becoming kindle for
Atmosphere without shelter near?

Luther Vandross said, "A house is not home."
Then the house is not a given, homes are built and made
Imagine music without a home, pictures, memories and rooms
    gone flicker flash
The musicians, artists, patrons, and good hard working family folk
Strived and saved for the house they earned
But just like these words become memory as Los Angeles
    music is heard
And this too shall burn . . .

                                                   – **A.K. Toney**

Catastrophe . . .

Some things cannot be fixed. Sharon's house: ash, silt, and
    memory.
    And her neighbor's house, and her neighbor's house,
and her neighbor's house down to the corner and round the block
    and down the block and further, all ash and silt and
    memory.

Left standing are chimneys built to contain fire, white ash-dust
    rising with each footstep over the cooled aftermath.
She wrote, "I have no words for this."
Neither do I, except to stand
    and hold her hand in this small way:
        Dear Sharon,
        It was my worst dread that your home was in grave danger.
        I am sorry —
        and greatly relieved you are safe.
        Love and friendship,
        Dan

– Dan Saucedo

The Ojai Fire

for our firefighters, the Forest Service
and for the residents of Pacific Palisades and Eaton Canyon

The mountains I love are covered with cinders
and for every cinder a world has died in the wilderness.
The sirens begin early, helicopters on the way.
Flames crest orange over the hills,
Fire flows down the riverbed.
I get off the plane from New York, return home
to fire leaping into the sky.
The moon rises red, a ruby in the night,
the sun dawns red in the morning
and the people who came to fight this
continue without rest.

The loss is to the mountains,
Matilija Canyon – burnt,
Wheeler Gorge – burnt,
Sisar Canyon, Casitas Pass, burning.
The fire burns into the night:
Black Mountain – 60% contained,
Carpinteria – 35% contained,
Wheeler Gorge – out of control
back beyond Beaver Camp,
crossing highway 33, around Rose Valley,
heading northwest to Lions Camp.
I watch the red snakes move up the mountainside.

Are the Chumash paintings burnt?
Are animals on fire, screeching in pain?
It is an angry mouth
breathing into the black sky

red beyond the horizon,
breathing into the clouds, anger and rage
burning around Ojai, Meiners Oaks, Santa Paula,
Lake Casitas, San Luis Obispo,
burning up Los Padres, Topa Topa, Sulfur Mountain.

The men are streaked black and weary.
They collapse into sleep,
but the fire rages on until the night of July 4th
when a cool fog rolls in.
The morning brings relief
with the cinders and devastation.

I mourn the loss,
the ghosts of dead animals echoing down the Topas.
Must every wild thing die in America?
Every deer in the wilderness?
Must every forest be slashed and burnt
dying from lack of care,
dying uncherished in ignorant America?
Does it stop at the silent horror of the Chumash
looking down at our valley?
Does it stop at a 60 foot wall of flame leaping
over our heads at the street corner?

– **Phoebe MacAdams**

A Sense of Urgency

Wind off the bay hurries grasses
from underfoot to the top of the hill,
where they pour down the opposite side
to climb again; rush to raise primitive
flowers that burgeon to seedhead.
Rustling impatiently in the wind's breath,
they're eager to release their seed
to gust, hide, trouser cuff.

A legion of tribes competes for an acre:
stately spires that vibrate in barely moving air;
coarser stubby stalks whose stiff brown heads
mimic pinecones.
                Withered in hot dry
climates, heavy dewfall stirs them
to send up shoots. Grasses can't wait.

Lying scorched on charred ground,
they're first to recover after a burn,
offer themselves up to restore the soil.
On the Plain of Abraham below
Mt. St. Helens, ash laid down
fifty feet deep left no living thing
where a year later, elk graze.

— **Cathie Sandstrom**

Non-Sonnet for Burning

First saw the embers on the television screen
Then saw the palm trees swaying in the high winds
Felt the car move side to side as tumbleweeds danced violently
Headed to the movies as planned the night before
Smelt the fire getting closer
Watched *Nosferatu* not realizing the evil force was outside
    the theater
Drove home to lights out and empty streets so eerie
A reminder of Covid silence times before
Tuned into the news and heard Eaton Canyon burning
Realized reality stood at our doorstep
Knocking then demanding for the land back
As the fire alerts and alarms wake us from slumber
All crying under masks, all coughing
Fire at our foothills, raging, always hungry for more

– Iris De Anda

Fire Ecology

Frequent fires are fueled by dry grasses
Ignited by a match, lightning or accident
Reacting to a circular set of relationships
Evolved over meteorological seasons

Ecosystems housing the wildland-urban interface
Conflagrate periodically due to climate whiplash
Organisms under this ecological architecture
Live reciprocally in a wilderness of biodiversity
Our human responsibility is to be more conscious
Geographic literacy honors ecological reality
You cannot deny that fire was here first

– Mike Sonksen

Ice and Fire

strange to
find myself here
in the deep freeze
while back there
the city burns
palisades reduced
to ash and ember
father texting in
a panic from
the assisted living
in pasadena
a mile or so outside
the evacuation zone
welcome to
southern california
i say once i reach him
feel relief to
hear him laugh

and then
as morning spreads
the uncertainty of
time zones
nearly nine am
in new york
still too early
to call either
him or rae
check in
with noah
out in riverside

where the winds
are cresting at
ninety-nine miles per hour
and every bit of static
every match strike
is a fire risk

how often have i joked
that being present
for disasters
such as northridge
made me an
angeleno
crucible by
quake or fire
flood or drought
so to be away
from home
on the opposite side
of the country
in that other city
i have long since
abandoned
what does that
make me now

– David L. Ulin

ghost town

i went to look
i wanted to see
where the gelson's had been
the market where in 1982 my boyfriend got a job
he showed up to for one week
but we lied to my mother saying he worked there for six
    months
we were living with her then, in west los angeles.
you can do that – live with your mom – when you aren't 21.
like my mother the gelson's is no longer there.
cancer took her. fire took gelson's.
she is spirit. gelson's, ghost town epicenter.
pacific palisades:
has no high school anymore.
how i wished i could go to pali high when i was a senior at uni.
if i went there, i thought, i would be pretty. i would be clean: a
    good girl.
the house my brother lived in—gone.
the rexall drug store where my mother bought my sister and i
    sand pails when i was three.
gone.
that apartment building where i did drugs when i was 16 – gone.
streets with one house left standing.
one beautiful home on an empty street.
a porch and a tree and rubble where laughter used to reside.
empty streets where kids used to play.
where parents parked their landrovers.
gone. gone. gone.

spirits looming, ghosts swirling
the sunsetting
hilltops and ocean views
plots of land
plots of land
plots of land
a house with lights on
a mercedes parked in driveway
closest neighbor two blocks away –
what are the sounds at night?

my mother is spirit; fire is ghost
memory swirls
street after street silent
but not still
ghosts rustle
silence: loud
if i stay too long on one block
staring at what used to be there
if i stay too long sitting in my car with motor running
all i hear
are the yesterdays.

– Nicca Ray

My Sadness is as Great as a Mountain: A Haibun

I was a two-year-old child lost in the seas of the aftermath of war; my family and I, Vietnamese boat refugees, who started a new life in Pasadena. Growing up in the City of Roses, I attended Marshall Fundamental Jr./Sr. High School and soon found my second home in the stones and stream that flowed through Eaton Canyon, where I learned to balance, jumping from rock to rock up the stream to the waterfall. In these mountains, I learned to fall and to get up again. Learned that sometimes climbing down was more difficult than climbing up, because gravity could make you slip. The oak trees and bay laurels wrapped their arms around my sadness and I felt loved. The deer taught me about the possibilities of life. The canyon gave me a silence that I could not find at home. The bird chirps offered me hope and joy, a counter to my father's PTSD and rage after fighting in the Vietnam War and spending nine years in a Vietcong prison. My family and I lost our Vietnamese Motherland and so much more. In these mountains, I found my other home. When the fires burned in Altadena in the New Year of 2025, my mountain burned down. The trees, trails and streams that offered me friendship, that strengthened my body, mind and spirit, not only in childhood but throughout my life, were engulfed in flames, as was my heart. The black bears, the squirrels, the deer ran frantically. The wings of birds caught on fire. Many friends lost their homes and many had to evacuate as the fire raced down the mountain. But I know, in time, the mountain will return again and so will we. Life, like pinecones opening to release seeds after a fire, will grow from the ashes. Indian paintbrush, mariposa lily, native chia, black sage, fire-followers.

my heart
the Santa Ana winds today
branches fall to the ground

— **Teresa Mei Chuc**

Perello Family's Journey to Re-Establish Our Lives
Go Fund Me, February 23, 2025

Dear friends and family,

Guess what?

We've moved into our new temporary home rental!

Thank God for remaining by our side and fearlessly placing yourself in our shoes and walking (sometimes crawling) this uncertain road, with us.

We're so grateful for your continued compassion, love, support, and willingness to place yourselves in our shoes, as we take this journey together. For "better or worse" indeed.

You are a source of strength for our family.

Special appreciation for friends and family, who understand what it's like to experience very rough times in life. Those deep valleys are something else. Pain knows pain. Did you find it?

Thank you for continuing to tirelessly lifting us up in so many aspects of our life. It has not gone un-noticed. You are seen, understood, valued, loved and appreciated.

In Gratitude,

> **– Ibarionex, Cynthia and our Sweet Furbaby, Gracie**

Water Hose Man

Don't cry for Victor Shaw
applaud what he did.
A black man who faced the inferno
with only a garden hose in his fist,
his gaze set on the abyss.
Victor fought like any man inside a war
protecting what his forefathers bled out to get
and held steadfast for 55 years.
Shaw embodied everything Altadena is.
Wiry as rebar, spawn of concrete and grit
weathered yet heroic and floorboard strong.
A man who went toe to toe
lashing Eaton's red jaw
with nothing but what amounts to spit.
Victor stood on Monterosa Drive
with something I sipped as a kid
giving up all the juice he had left.
Maybe his stream saved something,
something that hasn't been born yet.
An acorn. A fig leaf. Melodic cicada nests.
Maybe his efforts will blossom in Spring.
All I know, is when they found him
Victor had a smile on his face
as if his last efforts were not in vain.
But don't cry.
Maybe struggle was who this man was.
Maybe bravery was something that
flowed within Victor's veins.
Maybe ash and soot were
something he faced every day
fending off cactus and skunk

becoming machete in a land of weeds
hosing down mountains of charcoal
that rose every day.
The back taxes.
The chronic illness.
The vultures circling overhead
vying for him to sell it off cheap.
But some fights are worth a shot
be it your family
or the entire block.
Even if the deck is stacked.
Even if you burn both your ears.
Even if you're over your head
and the ending is clear
like water flowing over your hands.
But sometimes, you hold the line
give it all that you have.
Sometimes you fight until
all the sweat leaves your skin
holding on, holding the last weapon you possess
even if it's just a water hose in your hand.

– Pam Ward

Victor Shaw died protecting his family home in the Eaton Fire in Altadena, January 2025. Many of these homes are owned by multigenerational Black Angelenos. Pam Ward's family has lived in the Pasadena/Altadena area since 1904.

Ashes Over Angels

The hills are hollow now,
charred bones of trees reaching for a sky
too weary to rain
Smoke ghosts linger in the canyons,
whispering the names of the lost --
homes, memories, the coyote's den,
the old woman's rocking chair,
the child's red bicycle
Wind kicks up the ash,
a reminder that nothing rests,
not even ruin
Blackened palms stand like funeral torches,
burnt-out cars glint under an unforgiving sun
A dog howls in the distance,
searching for the life
that slipped through its paws
The city below still hums,
but the air tastes like grief,
like scorched earth and broken wings
They call it *resilience*,
this endless reclaiming,
this stubborn dance with disaster
But the land remembers
And someday, the flames will return,
hungry as ever,
to finish what they started

– **Richard Modiano**

Fire Head

When crouched down in the hills
surrounded by dried sagebrush
and golden wattle trees,
this is the story I imagine you tell yourself:

you were a colicky baby
breastfed on the Babylonic.
Built by fist and broken home,
your mother a junky,
your father, absent as the rent
that rarely got paid.

As a child,
you were bedwetter,
scrambled alphabet of loneliness,
inner world a bone ghetto
surrounded by broken mirrors,
and unmended fences.

As a teen,
whenever you stopped your lithium,
you were red-twitch
and phosphor-tongue,
smooth jazz
jammed into a light socket.

Then came that night
you set a downtown dumpster on fire,
the contraction in your chest
when *I love you*
was spelled out in smoke.

From then on,
what held you together—

potassium chlorate oxidizer,
fuel like sulfur,
wooden splint cut from aspen,
a binder like glue
creating a head that ignites
when struck against a rough surface.

As for your head:

Fire head. Fire awarded. Fire cracked.

One way to open pleasure
to the light, with fire.
One way to lessen the pain,
burn everything around you.

Whenever that irresistible urge
tapped into your vein like fuel,
you were rocket-ready
to enact every dangerous desire.

Now, crouched down in the hills,
surrounded by golden wattle trees
and dried sagebrush,
adrenaline drag races through your veins,
runs all stop signs.

Fever. Fervor.
Atlas of ignition.
Atman of ash.

You strike a match.
Your fingers like small rivers
bend around the flame,
cup it, keep it unmolested
from Santa Ana winds.

You pledge allegiance
to this flicker,
its yellow-mottled amber
seeping into your heart's
deepest blue.

You tell yourself
you are powerful, all-consuming,
that you can reduce
large areas of a lush and lavish city
to the dust
God chokes on.

– Rich Ferguson

Sudden

was the fire
like a wolf at a live heart

So many things
seemed filled with intent
to be lost

but the only lasting truth was change

and if you had a limitless
life
it would be a real problem

for you
Still

I wanted to come home
transformed

and be surprised
by the flickering

in our radically impermanent
robes

rain-soaked
and ringed with succulents

around
a tiled patio

where you'd put the fairy lights up

The mysterious nature of it—

all our rooms
all our ash

now a form in emptiness
to visit

Life
as it really is

The inconsolable
losses

The molten
heart

- **Michelle Bitting**

What Remains

A mug and a spoon
A baby book with photos
Found in the rubble

– Ellyn Maybe

Walking Home on 14th Street

Peripheral. First a whirring, then
pinkish glow, rising, like a strange
what? Horror movie in the almost-dark, sun-gone.

Crossing the freeway, that's when we see it,
a cotton-candy-colored plume and
bulbous, charcoal fumes above—
Smoke, I say, then god-fear,
Fire, must be fire!

West side of the street, it's coming up the embankment.
We're on the sidewalk, east side of the street.
Run to see. Prove I'm right. California poppy-yellow petals
in dark clumps of brush, fresh tongues of flame.

Dial 911.
14th near Olympic,
burning up hill toward the buildings.
On the west-bound, yes,
west-bound freeway bank.

A fire truck is here before I finish.
Wave them down, the phone voice says.
I'm in the street, flailing like a wind-whipped tree
in the siren-blaring, windless night.

Truck doors open, firefighters converge,
sizing up the scene. Three climb the chain-link fence.
Others drag out hoses, feed them up and over.
It's a job. Get it done. Pump-truck, ambulance,
everything in place.

Next day, a bald spot, hosed to ash and dirt, shows
where the burn had been; hardly anything
to notice. Dampness in the air. No wind.

No roadblocks. No water-dropping planes.
No startled animals. No burned cars. No one fleeing on foot.
No ruined hopes and dreams. No burned houses. No fallen trees.

If only all fires were like that.

– Hilda Weiss

L.A. Fires and Me

"A wall of flame," that's what my daughter saw
and so she fled to our house. No power here,
so she entered, the back door creaking, walked
back down the dark hall to her old room, a son
and daughter now in tow now, outside,
the wind howling.

Still no power. I am up oddly early, wondering
whether the electric blower works. It still does
and so I blow the porch and steps, no mask,
finding at the back door, a burnt fragment
of a page from a book, a fiction story about
a shipwreck, people lost at sea.

I will probably die of ash inhalation.
The air reeked of burning but then everyone
dies of something, don't they, though too soon
for my kids. Still no power. Every place is closed.
We look and look—McDonald's!
I have an Oreo milkshake for breakfast.

Her rental didn't burn but they were robbed--
took her son's computers and my daughter's
jewelry, though not the Bakelite bracelets
and only some money in her underwear drawer.
Now the owner wants to sell the place.
My daughter's chemo stayed on schedule.

– Marilyn N. Robertson

The Eaton Fire, Altadena, CA, January 7-8, 2025
for my daughter and son, who lost their homes

Like they all said
what you can do
is nothing.
The house will burn down
under the weight
of its own accumulated sunshine.
Tonight, windows knock about in their frames,
voices of generations calling
through the shattered glass.
Best not answer.
Let the trees cry out,
stripped of leaves
and hurling embers from their brittle branches.
Let the roof cry out,
the tar of shingles seething
through the cross beams.
Let the ceiling cry out
as it falls,
and the sprung piano,
in one last violent arpeggio.
And the books—
a bonfire of pages
swept miles afield
to settle in singed fragments,
incoherent as a foreign tongue.
Read nothing into the cryptic phrase
or the house untouched at the end of the block,
or the wedding ring in the sifted ash.
Only this:
Stand
where the scorched earth

still knows your footprint,
where vision drifts,
as always, to the mountainside,
now bare.
Let grief wash over you
like rain that did not come
to quench the flames.

– Mary Anne Berry

Mother Nature Talks Back

You agreed to give me
a fair warning
before you ooze
your steaming lava
or shake that tectonic thing
that makes buildings rumble
then tumble all over themselves
like that rent check
you try to ignore.

Some thought tornadoes
would have an effect,
but only Dorothy paid
attention and even then
I had to fling her Kansas
home somewhere
over a rainbow.

I told you I'm tired.

Woe is me, you cried
woe is you, I laughed
now we're cooking
with carbon monoxide!
Fooled you with my
nocturnal stealth.

                                                          –Laurel Ann Bogen

Oxygen

When the hills catch fire, the crews have no choice
but to attack from below. You don't want to be higher,

they say, that's how you feed yourself to it. Even so,
the fire can still fight back, loosening the ground

around trees and boulders, so they come crashing down.
The fighters learn this in fire school. Of course, it's harder

at night; they can only listen for whatever the fire may
drop. So, they go slow and call out to each other, Rock,

Tree, Animal. And since it's always night somewhere,
always out of control, one can imagine them right now,

walking up the dark like gods or children, naming
the world as it comes for them.

– **Brendan Constantine**

A Drive Along the Coast

In a dry age fires came
The coast is clear
We made love on Broad Beach
She tried to steal my ex-wife's jade necklace

Winds were in a religious fervour
Even though the white, clean body has gone,
Its ghost surfs north of the Malibu Pier
Where it learned to surf

The long row of beachfront houses burned down
Once the envy & the beauty visited
To live once, against the rebounding waves

In the age of dryness the phrase
"It behooves you to serve" was first heard
By a young sailor dressed in whites
With two black stripes on his sleeve

Even in a self-absorbed age
A man reaches out with minimum water
Even when there's no response,
He reaches out with water

– **Harry E. Northup**

A History of Fire Drills

one

She was our "live-in." My parents would throw parties and Dad's friends would get drunk and flirt with her in front of their wives. She was my babysitter. When we were alone in the house, she'd turn off the lights in her bedroom, turn on a spinning rainbow lamp and blast The Doors' first album. She'd invite me in and we'd dance wildly together. She was from Juárez. I was from Encino. She was seventeen. I was four. She was long and slinky, wore a white vinyl mini skirt and white go-go boots. I wore a flame-retardant blanket sleeper with a drop seat. Her boyfriend would knock on the side door, she'd sneak him in and send me back to my room. That was the year she got pregnant, 1967. Mom and Dad let her go and I never saw her again. "Light My Fire" became my first favorite song.

two

Flames rose from an empty lot at the end of our street. It was an open field full of shrubs and weeds. Helicopters circled above. We were all standing outside watching when a cop told us that my brother and his friend had been spotted lighting paper airplanes and releasing them into the brush. "We were making rocket ships," my brother later said. "We just wanted to see what would happen." It was 1972, the year of his Bar Mitzvah. He'd already failed his 8th grade aerodynamics elective. No homes burned, no one got hurt, but there was nothing left of the field. My dad got a bill in the mail for thousands of dollars, property damage. My brother's allowance was taken away, but just for a month.

three

The year I chose not to go to Jewish sleepaway camp was 1975, the summer of the Camp J.C.A./Barton Flats fire in the San Bernardino National Forest. My friends had to flee the scene in their pajamas. The next year, I switched to Camp J.C.A./Malibu because it felt safer. Decades later, *that camp* would be incinerated in the Woolsey Fire, along with Camp Hess Kramer and Gindling Hilltop Camp. Only the Torah scrolls survived.

four

We faced the wood-burning fireplace, legs pressed against each other, staring into the fire. He said, "There's a name for this: Tratak. It means *to gaze*. It's trance-inducing. Like an incantation. Like a drug you can take for free." It was 1978. No one was home. He could have easily kissed me. But he was a seeker. What was in front of him, never as compelling as what he could feel but not see. He knew things at sixteen that I have never learned.

five

There was a high-pressure system over the Great Basin. And me in an open-air Jeep. It was 1988, the year I turned twenty-five and dyed my hair party girl red. I flew through Rustic Canyon, one hand holding my hat on my head, the other on the wheel, holding a Marlboro Light. A gust of wind swerved the car. The cigarette dropped onto my leg, igniting my pantyhose, burning a smoke circle next to my knee. I've still got that burn mark.

six

Across the Arizona/New Mexico state line, we stopped at Phantom Fireworks. My husband stood next to the "Get The Party Started" assortment, as big as a bedroom wall. He debated. It was six hundred dollars. We settled on a smaller package and agreed, there would be enough bottle rockets to set off for the rest of our lives. It was 2008. Three weeks later, he'd be buried alive under twelve feet of snow.

seven

He'd once told me that *"when and if he died,"* to scatter his remains off a mountaintop. He was found frozen and was later cremated. I saved his ashes until 2018, wedged the temporary, cardboard urn deep in a bookshelf between Tom McGuane and Richard Ford. Sometimes I'd even forget he was there. It was my way of holding on, my way of letting go, my way of punishing him for leaving us.

eight

Last January, when my ninety-two-year-old mother had to evacuate her home in the San Fernando Valley, she came to Santa Monica to stay with us. She fell on our front steps and broke her shoulder. The doctor said it could "take a lifetime to heal."

nine

My friend's house is the only structure on her block that survived this year's Palisades Fire. Yet the smoke damage, the toxic fumes, make it impossible for her to return. She wants to take her house down to the studs, start over, same thing we both had to do when we first met, as widows in a grief group: rebuild—from the ground up. Her insurance company is forcing her to move back in. She calls herself "one of the left behinds."

ten

There was a chart of a Fire Exit Plan on our classroom wall. Whenever the alarm went off, we lined up single file and walked to the nearest exit and out the building. We weren't silent, we weren't orderly. We loved Fire Drills, a chance to practice escaping. What we didn't understand back in 1974 was, you can't simulate an emergency.

eleven

You could say that now, I am mostly numb. You could say, I miss my own fire.

– **Susan Hayden**

Equal Footing

In California, after his home
of 35 years burned to the ground
my pal Jan tried to keep
a positive attitude

Yesterday, two weeks after the fire
he was finally able to visit
the remains on a crystal clear
temperate California winter day

Fuck the sky
he wrote

Fuck California
Fuck Los Angeles

Underneath you could almost hear
the silent mutter
Why did this happen to me?

Jan—one of the kindest guys
in the world, the one who always called when visiting
to get together for pizza or a beer

Who donated a kidney to a friend in need

Who transported a Hammond organ
30 miles through horrific traffic
so he could play it for five minutes
at a poetry reading I hosted

The kind of guy who kept things:
ticket stubs, photos, programs
rare musical instruments
his own plays and poetry
all ash now overlaying
a broken foundation

Why did this happen to me?

Good friends are on equal footing
until lightning strikes—
cancer, dementia, divorce
fire

Losing everything

Now, what kind of footing are we on?
The routine is broken, the love remains

I just hope there is enough of it
to carry him through these dark days

– Kat Georges

Winds-Day

Woke up this morning, only to find
Wild winds enough to blow my mind!
Felt like Dorothy in the Land of Oz
Wind through my hair and dust in my schnozz!
Not used to those kinds of storms in L.A.
Trees pulled up from the ground lost their way
Back and forth swung the telephone wires
And miles from my house I spotted a fire
I knew then I had to leave home
But I didn't know just how far I would roam
The lights were all out, my cat under his chair
This wild, wintery Winds-day had us both scared
Through Thursday and Friday this Winds-day raged on
I was so afraid my city would be gone
But when I went back, my house still stood
I was glad that everything returned as it should
Tomorrow is Tuesday, and I'm not so sure
I want to experience another Winds-day anymore!

– Spencer L. Griffin

Snow Born from Flames

a soft song fills my ears and I can see a gentle breeze
    disturbing the trees
the air in the house is still, not yet having mixed with the wind
I step outside and as fresh air fills my lungs, an ache of
    discomfort and a wave of relief overtake me

the bulbs in the paper bags have all sprouted, the leaves yellow
    from a lack of sunlight
ash and dirt cover my hands as I bury the paperwhites further
    into the earth
I cover the soil with the leaves and flowers of seasons past,
allowing death to pave the way for life

as the sky begins to clear and unseen flames are put to rest
an uneasy peace fills our city as it slowly comes back to life
the ash falling from the sky has begun to settle,
creating a thin layer of off white on everything exposed to
    the sky

It may be January, but it will never get cold enough for
    morning frost here
this is the closest we will get to snow in L.A.

                                                      – Riot Renwick

It Seemed the Sea was Speaking in Tongues

        that only I could hear, hear
but not speak, not read. Its darkish waters and froth white
        as calcium rolled on the land, and it had warmed,
the sea, and its warming rhymed with warning, a warning
        I didn't understand.

Then they rose up, first one on the western side,
        then, on the eastern end, one more. *Fire*. Fires
clasped the city in between. And the fires were made
        not only of trees but of houses, not only of woodlands
but neighborhoods. The fires were made of appliances,

        frozen meats, plumbing and wiring, dogs and cats,
and the black tar of roadways. The fire in the west took
        storied homes that had hosted, once, beauties
and their fortunate men. The fire in the east burned paper,
        a manuscript of poems. A mini-mart, Open All Night,

burned all night and all day. It took, that fire, the profits
        made of paper, soft bills, handled
and handed. Over. The fires were made of toys.

Once, a boy of just four had a small bear. (The reader,
if there is one, should picture little overalls, the bear's.)
When the boy looked in his shiny black eyes, they
gazed back. They *saw* him. He was a lonely boy.
It was taken, that bear, as gone as if by fire.
At age 90, he remembered, still. That boy was my father.
        The fires weren't made of memory, memory
doesn't burn. Memories die but don't burn. People burn
        through money, burn bridges, burn for justice

or revenge. They burn their candles at both ends.
      Newspapers burned with their stories of a young man
who couldn't walk—palsy. He waited in bed for his mother
      to return, then waited for the flames.

Once, a mother told her girl, quite suddenly
she did, then never mentioned it again, Next time
the world will end in fire. This mother knew the Bible
but kept it to herself—with her thoughts. All but the most
sudden. Her silence spoke. Rather like the sea she
was deep. I was that girl.

The sky turned a deeper grey, the air breathed smoke.
      The land's gone a bit too dry, cities to kindling.
The sea had warned me. The sea had spoken in tongues
      and bones, the ribs of shipwrecked sailors hunting
whales for oil. For light. The sea stroked them 'til
      they drowned. It made of them grains
for its beaches. The sea had warned me—it knows

      nothing. Water knows fire, nothing
knows it better. Something's wrong, no doubt, something
      always is. The sea warmed and warned. I listened
but could not understand. And the others? They
      are millions, tens of. One billion. No. They be
more. They be many more than that.
      They don't even listen.

- Suzanne Lummis

Canyon Country

Fog shrouds eucalyptus—
lank crowns, morning crowns
eucalyptus clothed
in fog, then fire.
No guitar is made from eucalyptus
—the finger's flight along the strings
would ignite the frets.
But a guitar, made of alder,
trembles resonantly
as eucalyptus burns
its paper skin curling into black,
a burning book.
Smoke climbs into eucalyptus
branches hand over hand.
A crow cries out, the shrouded flock
flutters, the house of crow
hot with eucalyptine arson
burning joist and cross-beam—
a guitar, made of alder-wood,
finds a minor chord, a
broken eucalyptic chord
a broken cindered eucalyptus
chord, an elder chord,
a fire-season chord, a
sympathetic chord
that calls downslope
to an impassive tide.
Made of alder, the instrument's
open eye widens.

Eucalyptus burns,
the minor broken wooden chord
burnt until its mouth
can say nothing legible.

– **Tom Laichas**

Wild Fire

This house has two windows
And I, like a migrant,
Move between them
To escape the burning sun.

In the morning, I sit at the northern window
And repair poetry
With my talking computer.
In the evening, I go to the southern window
Sit on my rocking chair
And listen to my talking book.

But today, the air has fever
Like a swollen body,*
The sun is an ugly wound**
Opening its mouth
And the house smells of smoke.

A fire has caught the skirt of the city.
Right now, hundreds of firefighters
Are engaging with the wild fire
In groves, canyons and towns,
And thousands of homeless men, women and children
Have moved to shelters
With their horses, dogs and cats.

I wish it would rain.
Then I could sit
At this window sometimes
And sometimes at the other one
And listen to the sound of the rain
Falling equally over houses,
Both burned and unburned.

– Majid Naficy

* *From "It Is Night", a poem written by the Iranian poet Nima Yushij.*
** *From "Prose of Trans-Siberian", a poem written by the Swiss poet Blaise Cendrars.*

What I Didn't Lose in the Great L.A. Fires

Fire's really close, yells S., my youngest son, seventeen, to me.

He spins from where he is standing with his therapist on our house's wraparound driveway, jumps to the kitchen window where I'm at the kitchen sink washing dishes. He presses his nose, cheeks and chin into the window's old screen material until I stop and give him a meaningful look. His profile still in the screen is distinct—yet, invisible—anguished and suspended in front of me.

He runs away, gravel spits under his heels spits like mad bees tearing from a bee's nest.

We gotta go now! S. yells, grabbing the kitchen screen door which slaps the house like a palm to forehead brow slap.

S. stands in the middle of our dim kitchen, leaning against the thick cracked grey marble that sits on top of the old school table I found at the hospital thrift. He looks dazed like he's lost—like he doesn't recognize me—like he's a weathervane that's stuck on south. He shakes himself awake, sees me.

We gotta go now Mom! My son pivots and runs outside again to watch the eastern sky.

Can I get a signature, my son's young para-therapist asks walking into the kitchen, *You might want to uh--go.*

Huh?

Now look Mom! yells S. from outside.

It just looks close, I shout, *Really, fire's far away—like an optical illusion.*

Better get him out of here, says M., my husband and son's father, from behind me where he stands in the open refrigerator lighted by the unit's light where he holds the package of cellophane-wrapped salmon I just picked up at Whole Foods up to his nose, sniffs it and tosses it onto the vintage metal sink counter next to me.

I groan, throw the yellow sponge that I'm using into the old sink hitting the hole in the drain that my husband fixed with a large nut and a red nickel-sized rubber washer. I dart for my bedroom, a large simple room with cloud lift beams that was our house's former living room architect Henry Greene designed and attached to 1910 wood milking sheds in 1924. I stand at my bedroom doorway, looking left and right, hapless as my eyes skim over a room I used for a studio and well, everything it takes when art is your everything—when you're an artist, a mom and poem maker—like it's your zip code.

Racks and bins of raffia, premium and cheap thread, yarn, saved bits of gift and spools of expensive couture dress ribbon are jammed and double-parked with books—read and mean to read—design, poetry and classics, memoirs, self-help, autism with samples of my couture sewing and weaving attempts.

Overhead hangs one of a pair of matching cream-colored hand-painted silk pendants that my husband and I imported from Murano that look like Star Trek starships over the years of art finds—a pair of '40s fruitwood postmodern Danish klismos, a curved '50s sofa from a studio's warehouse's cleanout that a friend vendor from France put on a diet to give it Hollywood curves and sexy legs before he recovered it with a rare remnant of the watermarked sage silk velvet he'd been saving that I could never have afforded otherwise.

As for art—sheesh—my room is hung gallery style—art over art—like a Louvre for kid paintings inter-hung with my ironic comic temperas, oversized oil paintings of rose bouquets, the Gamble House, found art, sticks and strings, a tornado of art and weavings mixed with the black and white portrait photographs from when my husband and I became new parents—again—at forty-six when we adopted our youngest, S.. Photos of our son as a newborns and with his brother, A. as a graduate and the cache of no reason photos of us being pretty and not—and the few we have of our beloved long gone ancestors.

One is of S. and I on the highbacked sofa I designed for The Pasadena Showhouse to resemble a garden hedge that's embedded with a circle like a certain Renaissance Madonna and Son sit framed inside a halo—albeit this one an oaken one and somewhat dropped—and not nearly as saintly—yet, somehow fitting.

Next to me is a rack of vintage clothes that's mixed in with newer near stacks of antique Fortuny remnants and boxes of Victorian jet beads, exquisite flaxen lace embroideries—museum stuff—thin as new baby hair—a Swedish widow who'd just immigrated to Kentucky made or, so said the vendor who sold it to me espoused. Women who knew how to do things—start over things—but as foreigners, all alone, hitting the plains—who get things done with a needle or plow, demolished or not, who could spin gold from straw!

Nearby, other confections—or starts to some big ideas—why I kept them—like a magpie stockpiling plaids that someone likely Amish spent their life hours over—folded linen like linenfold in a church pew—trimmed on the bias, folded in both selvages into 3/4" strips and ironed super flat as copier paper before the maker rolled her material into three fat softballs—and then, what? Fed her baby! A cow! Went to market. I don't know what! And I don't know what to take!

Take the five spools of extra wide black vintage grosgrain hat ribbon—the good kind—the British or French kind—that I absconded with from some granny Midwest garage that I keep tucked in a drawer under a drawer of Bakelite buttons—of acorns, twigs, owls, birds—and packages of still wrapped felting needles, my mother's scissors, cream silk layette blanket binding, leather and metal thimbles and sewing needles.

All of it culled—no, dare I say, curated—by a queen of stuff—the queen of beginning again as a mother again, of her hard start son and now under threat of fire! Aka *Queen Mother Interruptus.* A special needs mom who can hardly think who, instead of making art or writing poems, ruminates on what could ease her new son's rage, his birth trauma, adoption trauma, autism, fetal alcohol syndrome, woo him?

The stuff of therapy stuff besides the stuff in the room!

I look around me not knowing where to begin now—spot a long green and purple silk dirndl that designer Peter Lam made that I got from his shop on Mission in San Marino. See more goodies from the Rose Bowl, Pasadena City College's flea or that trip I insisted upon with my husband that we took with our then five-year-old firstborn towhead son when we joined my older brother and his partner in the South of France and day-tripped to the Il Sorgue Flea.

I swoon!

Stuff that I now keep like a wallflower waiting to be asked to dance, *goose-stuffed* into the pair of ceiling high white oak two bookcases that I bought for a song from the old Saks' Women's Shoes when the department store gave up on Pasadena and held a fixtures sale.

Opposite sits a dress mannequin that wears the bodice cape I made when motherhood kicked me and my arrogance about mothering to the curb when I was a *motherwreck* mother ship—a shipwrecked ghost ship. When, as far as art, all I could do was make knots—square knots—in *chop water, carry wood* fashion—I mean, *chop wood, carry water*—in threads, shred of do overs, rip outs, add ons, circle backs that only got better with all the starts and stops of mothering, buying time to bond with our new son and figure his needs.

Experiments that grew—like our boys—over the years. Six years of knots—or in paint strokes made like hidden measures in chenille, cashmere, wool, inside out silver coffee packaging, plastic, glitter, my unrepairable Anne Klein navy velvet pants and twine for a downline version of angel wings—aka Durer's watercolor of an European Roller—that when doubled became an ancient prow statue—*Winged Victory of Samothrace*: *Nike* that's installed at the Louvre. I'm ancient too now with a pair of wings in the cape I made that was as much a cry for help for peace! Earth! In polychrome how the original was made. What reminds me I can do hard things—well—*well-ish*--if I commit to mistakes as wayfinding and can survive things.

Mom! My son runs into me, *What do I do? What do I pack?*

I spot a dry cleaner's plastic bag in the trash, knot an end and hand it to him, *Here! Fill it with what you want to take!*

He speeds away down our house's dark tunnel hall. I pull the bodice cape off the mannequin, push it into a large blue IKEA bag, see the leather and brass claw my oldest son made when his freshman art teacher gave him a second shot instead of failing him sparkling on my desk and shove it the bag.

Forget all about my steel grey Prada trench that's perfect for a sexy noir romp that's scattered with all-over pink silver dollars. Forget too, the black Gautier slinky number that I wore to my dad's funeral. Forget my old man too while I'm at it—Dad a white, cold, untouchable giant avalanche--so still when I last saw him, I had to poke him to be sure he was gone. The man my older sister must have had dressed in the new itchy navy Big Man Tall Man suit Dad was wearing. Forget you too Dad! Forget I ran to my car to return with my makeup bag before the undertaker saw me when I started Dad's makeover. Put my overcoat on to make myself big—hid me and my masterpiece—Dad as my canvas I painted him alive again with Maybelline's City Bronzer and Contour and floured Dad back. Here again. But happy looking solid gold–San Tropez gold.

Across from me in my bedroom sits the so-called *important* table that the postmodern antiques dealer who sold it to me said, *Was by Mario Bellini—I'm sure of it—is worth millions—well, would be if it was signed.*

On top of it sits my first poetry manuscript with the books I'm reading. I shove them into my *Votes for Women* tote. Open a cupboard, spot the photo album my son's birthmother sent to show our son's Kentucky family along with the small book of candid photos from our wedding.

I look down at what I'm wearing—half an old *Yohji Yamamoto* men's suit—the jacket I bought in Soho at a sidewalk sale 40 years ago—I grab the pants, a twenty year old *Etro* men's houndstooth sportscoat, grab my Estradiol hormone cream, my laptop and the now filled IKEA bag and stand in the doorway looking back at my stuff. Sixty-five years as a magpie collector.

I run to the hall safe--grab our passports, my husband's Rolex and a silver Spratling jug from when we had dough, a manila file with marriage, divorce and death certificates, my grandmother's Irish born certificates with my newly-minted Irish citizenship certificate.

Time to go, I yell to my son.

No answer. I check outside, see my son is in the back my '06 Camry (our oldest son is already out, unaware of our emergency exodus). Seeing my young son's medicine bag on top of the microwave, I grab it and stuff it into the IKEA bag.

You're leaving soon too, right? I ask my husband who's unwrapping the salmon package on the sink counter and sniffing it.

I'm deciding whether there's enough time to cook dinner. I'm already packed for my Dallas trip tomorrow and still want to grab a few things, then I'm going, he says.

Okay, I'll text you as soon as I find a hotel, I say, pushing open the kitchen screen door, turning to my husband, spotting the books I had been reading earlier that are still on the kitchen table. I put the books under my arm and run to the car where my son clutches the plastic sack that I gave him in the rear seat that he's filled with stuffed lovies and the new basketball, *Twister* game and *Jenga* he got for Christmas.

I toss my books on the passenger seat and get, drive my car past our house and stop at the top of the narrow drive to the upper cul de sac where I see my neighbors leaving—mass pandemonium—as their cars move forward and backwards, around and around the cul de sac, making three-point turns.

Too many cars, too many maneuvers at once done by people who know how to drive—who've forgotten how to drive!

On a far-off hill the night sky off—looks like a bull gored and bled out—glows alizarin crimson and burnt sienna is *painterly*, shot through with a skidding drybrush over the cosmos in cadmium orange. Rough handling done in paint but with a boar's bristle—a Fuller man's hairbrush—where there should be deepening dusk, stars and mountains of tree points and chaparral in evening dress and shadows. What's become more of a Turner sky—a torqued sky—a mad sky. A furnace that's hellbent on freefall charring our cupped landscape in the foothills like so many black Pickup Sticks falling in on each other like the masts of empty tall ships—stricken by a plague—ghost ships battling ghost ships—or pirate ships--indefensible on a pitched sea being whipped by hurricane winds.

Mom! We gotta go! Drive!

Okay! I say to my son as I drive and dial The Hilton and get India and sweettalk us into the hotel's last room.

The cul de sac streetlight comes on over my car. It lights the books on the passenger seat next to me. James Baldwin's *The Fire Next Time*, Ed Hirsch's *100 Poems to Break Your Heart*, Marie Howe's *What the Living Do*. Titles that may be Altadena's last words—or our first in years after so many unknowns, mistakes and miscalculations—it's in the making, beginning again, finding trust—the light that may come afterwards.

- Maryrose Smyth

4 Haiku

dark skies tinged with red
painted by embers and ash
loom ominously

as neighborhoods burn
permanence becomes fragile
while years turn to ash

in the midst of flames
memories are devoured
and hearts are broken

on the phone she cries
while telling me what happened
to all that she lost

– Land Flowers

Fire Roulette

Roulette is played by trigger-happy wind
that carries sparks to desiccated fuel.
A flaming skull of fire launches ash.

The lethal embers carried through the air
are infiltrating timber in their path.
Roulette is played by trigger-happy wind

that hits its mark and burns a canopy.
The branches, leaves, and trunk go up in smoke.
A flaming skull of fire launches ash,

ignites my thirsting space. The driving thrust
that lights a match, familiar brazen risk,
roulette a game of trigger-happy wind.

A company of fighters puts it out,
their arms around the house to help it stand.
A flaming skull of fire launches ash.

The haze will shroud my mind's aridity.
First douse the cinders so they do not catch.

Roulette is played by trigger-happy wind.
A flaming skull of fire launches ash.

– Jeanette Clough

Perello Family's Journey to Re-Establish Our Lives
Go Fund Me, March 17, 2025

I am writing to you today with a very grateful yet heavy heart.

On January 7, 2025, our beloved home in Altadena, California, was completely destroyed by the Eaton wildfires. It wasn't just a building; it was a sanctuary filled with love, forgiveness, and memories of years of hard work and resilience. The pain of losing everything is unbearable, and we're struggling to find our way forward.

We have lost everything. The only thing we had when we fled our home was the shoes on our feet, my purse, our pajamas, three framed photos, my youngest sister Jacquelyn's urn, and the urns from three of our fur babies who crossed over the rainbow.

My wedding dress is what I think of the most. It was destroyed in the fire.

The recovery process will be long and tough. We've been displaced three times: first, the night of the fire, we fled to the Pasadena Convention Center wildfire evacuation site with our three-year-old dog Gracie, my eldest sister Saundra and her 17-year-old dog Bosco, and my husband. We all ended up in a tiny hotel room for almost a month (which cost us a fortune out-of-pocket) and then a friend helped us out at a more affordable Airbnb in Atwater for another month.

Finding a temporary place to live was a real challenge, especially with the high demand for housing. After searching everywhere, we finally found a small rental on February 22, 2025. We have a 2 year road (or more) ahead of us and we need your continued support.

If compelled, please feel free to donate (or even donate again!) whatever you can to our GoFundMe page to help us with establishing our life. And please feel free to share this with anybody that might be able to assist.

No sum is too small or too much.

We have a long distance to getting back to any type of normal life.

We are starting from ground zero.

Thank you for your love and various levels of support.

– The Perello Family

A New Plague

> *Moses raised his staff toward heaven. God gave forth thunder and hail, and fire came down to the ground inside the hail, and God rained down hail over Egypt.* – Exodus 9:23

I don't like thinking about plagues in January
but everything is against me. Open up any Torah

to its current page and it's nothing but plagues.
If you're not a believer, open your Los Angeles window

or turn on any electronic device to see
the fire has left from inside the hail.

It is on its own now, inventing a punishment
no one deserves. The land of Goshen is spared

but sparse in Southern California and I'm
lucky enough to live in one sliver of it.

Our bags were packed just in case.
Our documents put in a folder so we could

prove whatever needed to be proved.
The cat carriers in the middle of the floor.

Text messages from the entire diaspora
wondering if we're okay. Pasadena, where I

received a Torah in book form in 1984
burned to the ground. Pacific Palisades,

one of our paradises, now a thing of the past.
A new plague has blown into Southern California.

I don't know who Pharaoh is in this metaphor
but I know we need to be let go.

Please.
Let us go.

– Rick Lupert

Something Thrown Away

The dogs upstairs are whirling around the living room
again. The green fruit hangs like a set of ornaments.

Heat presses me further into the sofa.
Tiny wind.

Now the air is ripped
by the breath of a passing helicopter.
Someone smashes eggshells on the counter
in another room.

Somehow, it is night again and I haven't seen it fall.
In the quiet summer moonlight, there is snow
on the banister. Ivy falls
across the wooden staircase to the deck.

This is what I plan to do:
I'll put on my black wool coat
and walk across the patio,
barefoot on cement.

It could be any season.

Rush of water as if the house
is taking a long shower.

A slight chill.
Bushes of stars. Wilting.
From a long way up:

dry avocado leaf
falling like a carefully delivered gift.

Eucalyptus flickers into the car.
It is hard to steer. I lose my bearings
somewhere after the first baseball field.
The cat is bored, beside me.
Sophisticated, in her cage.

Through the drooping, tired trees,
sunset spreads like a bruise.

It is as though the fire leaps from the valley to the top of the
    mountain.
Like an angry curtain.
This is the view.
The pump is broken.

I don't know where the stars are.
There is an unwanted call.

– Sarah Maclay

Shockproof

This was published as a social media post on January 9, 2025, two days after the first fires broke out in Los Angeles. I suppose I could sit down and write something that is more artful, but I think what I put down in the midst of all Hell breaking loose has an immediacy I would not be able to capture from a remove. I am, after all, a journalist. I have not changed a word.

"The Fire Show" was my name for the wall-to-wall all-night coverage of the blazes.

Late yesterday afternoon, I was on the phone with one of my oldest friends in L.A., whose home in Pacific Palisades burned to the ground on Tuesday. "Is there anything I can do?" I asked. He replied, "Can you replace my record collection?"

Not long after this conversation, "The Fire Show" on KTLA announced that the Sunset fire had broken out near Runyon Canyon low in the Hollywood hills. The video was terrifying. I called a friend of mine and learned that the lunatic was standing at Curson and Fountain, mere blocks from the blaze, where he had ridden on his bike, and he said it was cooking. The streets heading south were in total gridlock caused by fleeing residents. Looking at the wind-driven fireball on the screen, I determined that the fire could burn right through my neighborhood just like the other fast-moving conflagrations here in town, and it was time to get the fuck out of Dodge. With no plan in mind, I threw my birth certificate, expired passport, a laptop, a digital recorder, notebooks, and a few days' worth of clothing into a bag. No one I know in my 'hood could be raised on the phone. I said to hell with it and headed out the door on foot, passing a crackhead with what appeared to be a .45 automatic in his hand on my way to the express bus stop. I got out at Western Avenue, with a notion of going to

Union Station, but on the phone my onetime significant other sternly and reasonably suggested that I call our mutual friend Blackie. He answered the call and scooped me up within minutes, and we rolled downtown.

Blackie repairs and builds amplifiers under the business handle Shockproof. (He took the name, and his logo, from a 1949 film noir shot partially in the nearby Bradbury Building by director Douglas Sirk.) He works in an office/apartment not far from City Hall, and not far from Skid Row. We watched a bit of "The Fire Show" and I crashed on an inflatable mattress, surrounded by great gear. This morning, after an anxiety-filled night of fitful sleep, I awakened to learn that the Sunset fire evacuation order had been lifted. At Blackie's suggestion, we headed out through the amber air to Nick's, a DTLA diner that is a traditional hangout for the local railroad men. Just sitting for an hour in this restfully backdated relic of a largely vanished city was a tonic after two days of destruction, apprehension, and fear.

I was deposited in the Miracle Mile and unpacked, but the bag is still out; local high winds are presently predicted for early next week. This afternoon, I'm going to settle in with a good book. Let me know if Blackie can fix your ailing amp and I'll send along his info. Dude is a hero of mine forever.

– Chris Morris

Singed Memories

There are places I water
with my wanderlust; a once upon a time first date,
where ice cream and insecurity crept up my breast after an
    open party in Bel Air.
He was caramel skinned with cornrows – just a touch above
    my paygrade.
His beauty was a dream and a reckoning, that I was just the
    right *umpf,* enough for his cocoa lips, golden eye rolls, and
    depth of unveiling.
The: who he was, what he's done, whatcha gonna be, chatter.
I was just fixated on the exactness of that moment; this
    gorgeous Black man, on a sweet little stop with me in the
    Palisades Village.
Not my stomping grounds, but one he seemed to verge into
    familiar.
I wanted more:
of the ice cream
of his promised kisses
of the buttoned tight neighborhood
of this random party exchange,
but my number went mute.
Like the chirping birds from each puffed treetop
like the walls that held phone calls and songs
like the arches that brought out the most vintage charm
like the dream of my baby eyes
experiencing all the randomness of these young womxn's
    curves.

I wish it would have all come again,
though my diminished hope shed its last sigh of skin
along the tendrils of my ashen hair,
with ends split like the doorways to so many firsts
that will forever be hardened to that once memory
and wanderlust of uncertain delicacies.

– Jessica M. Wilson

If all my dreams had come true
I would've been living in Malibu or the Palisades
I would've lost everything

– kamla maya

State Farm Said to Keep a Journal but I Wrote a Poem Instead

I

I can't say I was completely surprised after two unnerving days of historic Santa Ana winds and lost power. Conditions were bad: severe drought, low humidity, dry brush, a violent windstorm and faulty power lines.

Fire broke out at 6:18 pm. We were eating dinner when we got the orders. Nicky, our son, and Yuka, his fiancée, could see the fire coming towards our house from their balcony. And immediately after, at 7:24 pm., an urgent text from emergency services.

Fast-moving wildfire in your area. An evacuation order has been issued. Leave now.

Burning brush fueled by high winds and flames heading towards the houses in northwest Altadena. We got the cat into her carrier. And then rushed around grabbing medicine and other necessities. Nicky and Yuka secured Cha Cha and gathered key items. Nicky was intent on saving as much music equipment as he could and made trip after trip to his car. I kept saying *We have to leave now. Right now.*

What do we call the day after the Day of the Epiphany?

At 6:26 p.m. all firefighters were called to report for duty.

At 7:30 p.m. all firefighting aircraft were grounded due to strong and dangerous winds.

II

Traffic was slow on our way down Lake, so many neighbors clearing out at once. I got on the phone to find us rooms. I booked the last spot at the Marriott in downtown Pasadena for Tom and me and found a room for the kids at Howard Johnson's on Colorado across the street from Pasadena City College. The kids checked in while Tom and I went to find a place to buy cat food, litter, bowls, drinking water, flashlights and N95 masks.

Many streets were dark due to outages, and trees and power lines were down. The air was filled with smoke and ash and the wind was so strong it was practically impossible to get in or out of the car. Once out of the car it was hard to walk a straight line in the battering wind. Most stores were closed. They'd either lost power or were too filled with smoke to be safe. But Ralph's was open.

When we arrived at the Marriott there was a long line to check in. Most of the guests were there with one or more dogs or cats. Over our week there it was our sad little haven. It smelled like smoke. But we were safe and every ride up or down in the elevator involved an exchange with fellow evacuees about whether their houses still stood. Over the days more and more first responders arrived from California cities north and south and from other states. There was a long line of firetrucks parked in front of the hotel facing north, facing the fire. We thanked and blessed the first responders whenever we could.

By five in the morning the Eaton fire had reached 1,000 acres and 100 mile per hour winds were clocked at one spot in the San Gabriel Mountains. In other parts of the valley winds reached 80 and 90 miles per hour.

III

We got a call from the kids just after 9 a.m. telling us they hadn't been able to sleep. They'd decided sometime between four and five a.m. to drive up and check on the house. When they arrived, it looked from the street as though our property was completely on fire. There were no fire trucks on our block or anywhere else to be found. Nicky said it looked like a warzone. When they got closer, they could see that while our houses were still intact the two houses directly behind us were engulfed in flames and small fires were beginning to burn on our side of the back wall.

The telephone pole began to smoke and Nicky grabbed a garden hose and with its very low pressure tried to keep the embers from spreading. He called 911 multiple times but they said they were overwhelmed and would come when they could. The winds began to pick up towards them and they thought it was time to get the fuck out. I've seen the videos: The sky is a smokey orange and the fire itself a blinding brilliance. In one video you can hear the sound of Yuka running back from the street to Nicky in the backyard. She says in a sweet urgent tone *We should get out, baby! They're not coming!"*

But just then the winds suddenly shifted direction and Nicky and Yuka continued to spray down what they could. Two high school boys jumped over the wall to the north—boys we'd never met, boys a neighbor told us later were "St. Francis lads"—and asked if they could help. The four of them fought off the spreading fire for four or five hours and managed to save our house, the kids' back house, the house to the north and two houses to the south. The neighbors across the street saved their houses as well. But the street behind us was completely destroyed for blocks and blocks and our street, starting about five doors up, is mostly gone. Nicky said when the firefighters finally showed up after about four hours they discovered that the hydrant directly in front of our house was not working. We later learned the system was out of water.

Nicky and Yuka determined it was safe to leave for the time being and braved the downed electrical lines and burning houses and cars all along the route to check on Yuka's sister's house further up in Altadena. They discovered complete devastation in Kiko and John's neighborhood. And there, too, not a firetruck anywhere in sight.

Mom, we didn't tell you we were going because you would have worried. And told us not to go.

They did call Yuka's mom in Japan. Yae is a devout Buddhist and prayed like crazy right about the time the wind changed in their favor.

IV

Over the next days I watched and re-watched the videos the kids posted on Instagram. I could see the houses behind us engulfed in flames and hear the wild crackling of the fire and the sound of fierce wind battering the awning of our back house. In the far distance a lone siren. At one point the wind picks up and our windchimes ring out a frantic tune accompanied by a kind of unexplainable rattle as the buildings come down just over our back wall. Sparkling embers are carried on the wind and flicker in the sky near the tallest branches of the oaks and the pine.

I watch the drive up to Kiko's. On both sides of the road orange and yellow flames lap at building after building. The smoke is thick and black and the trees appear petrified in the ashen light. When they reach Kiko's block you can hear the emotion in their voices. *Oh, my God. Literally all gone. The street is all gone.*

All that remains: Rubble, the most resilient of the trees, chimneys, fireplaces, an occasional burned-out car. The landscape looks carpet-bombed. Many have said it. It also looks like a moody painting from another century rendered in every shade of mist and gray.

I replay the one where you hear Yuka ask Nicky if he has a mask. When they get out of the car at what was once Kiko's you hear the pain in their voices. Yuka says *I'm so sorry. I'm so sorry.*

In the next video they're driving back down the hill and you can see billowing black smoke and the blackened skeletons of businesses and cars on North Lake. At one juncture there's a row of parked firetrucks. Lights flashing but trucks going nowhere. We later learn the firefighters were ordered to stand down because the winds made it unsafe for them to go in. The fear was that many of them might have been lost in a futile battle against the flames. The fire was contained at last on January 31st.

V

We're almost three months in, and the feelings don't go away. They shift and change and come around again. They say we're the lucky ones. Because our house still stands. But we are one house away from destruction and have much remediation to do from smoke, soot and ash which contains an unprecedented amount of toxic chemicals. Urban firestorms are not the same as wildfires. They say it will be years before it's truly safe again.

We have much business to do with State Farm and Service Masters, FEMA and the Army Corps of Engineers, the environmental abatement company, the public adjuster and a law firm which is mounting a *mass torte* lawsuit against Southern California Edison. Daily calls with Gina, Lena, David, Joshua, Kipp and others. Tom and Nicky have made forays into the houses wearing hazmat suits, meeting with agents and mediators and restorers who've told us to prepare to part with many treasures. Anything permeable is at risk. They have taken every last thing out of the houses to determine what can be salvaged and at some point they will tear out insulation and set up an ozone machine and do a power-clean inside. Outside, the Army Corps will clear debris and replace six inches of topsoil.

We've seen where we are on the new map outlining fire danger zones. It resembles a red ring of fire. We sit right on the border. We've seen our neighborhood on Google, our house on the edge of rubble. We can see the devastation on the streets directly behind us, just over our back wall, burned to the ground house after house for blocks and blocks and blocks. We hear the reports of looters and squatters in our neighborhood.

We're in our fifth rental since the fire. The month of February we stayed at Juan Carlos and Alicia's beach house in Oxnard eight houses up from the naval station at Port Hueneme. There was a bar next door called Beachcombers' Tavern, a friendly place to watch the Super Bowl and take in old George's crazy card tricks at the bar. One night from the deck we watched a SpaceX rocket arc over the water after taking off from Vandenberg Air Force Base. There was a small second story TV room where we had a view of the ocean and I'd sit there with the cat on cold days soaking up the colors of sand, sea and sky. But I couldn't sleep at night. I learned that they test oversized unmanned underwater submarines at the naval station, just a football field away from us, in the middle of the night, and the low-level beeps and high-pitched tones and muffled thumps and rhythmic ticking infiltrated my rest.

We fight about whether to return to our house at the end of the year or move on. There is so much to lose. So much that has been lost. We call ourselves refugees. But life in exile is not all bad. All of our community cats are safe and accounted for. I contacted Allison, who lived in the house directly behind us. They plan to rebuild. By some miracle they were able to grab the semi-feral kitty we call Charlie and take him with them to a hotel. She sent me a picture of him curled up on the bed of their hotel room and I cried with relief.

At this new spot, where we'll stay for the rest of the year, there are no birds. Altadena was a bird paradise, and we miss our wildlife there and our trees and our flowers. Our cat, Mimi, seemed bored. We put on cat TV a few days ago and haven't turned it off. She's made friends with these virtual visitors, especially excited by the large mourning doves, blue jays and squirrels. Our moods, too, have since improved.

Tom broke his foot last week, but life goes on. We took an Uber to Little Tokyo on Saturday night to see Nicky and his band open for sax player Yasuaki Shimizu at the Japanese American Community Center. Riding past the homeless encampment along San Pedro Street downtown was bracing. The man who drove us home was an injured veteran of the Iraq war. He said his Humvee blew up outside of Fallujah. He made sure we put on our seatbelts. The show was a revelation.

These days we're occupied with the business of living. We are busy staying alive. If you asked me how I'm doing right now I would say I'm not without hope.

– **Lin Nelson Benedek**

Perello Family's Journey to Re-Establish Our Lives
Go Fund Me, July 1, 2025

Dear friends and family,

Ahhh! It finally arrived!

As most of you know, our beloved and cherished home completely burned to the ground caused by the Altadena/Eaton wildfire, January 2025.

This catastrophic loss has deeply impacted our family, both materially and emotionally. In addition to losing our home, we lost irreplaceable items of deep personal and cultural significance: My wedding dress, my husband's professional photography equipment, one of many photography awards which includes recognition from IPC awarding him at the United Nations, Delegates Room in New York City as one of the top photographers in the US, along with so many other sentiments and inspiring items representing hard work, dedication, commitment, heart and soul and in our lives. The devastation has been overwhelming. The emotional toll cannot be overstated from the deep loss we experienced together.

Well, this afternoon Ibarionex received a FedEx package from IPC (perfectly framed, etc.) with another award to replace the one destroyed in the wildfires. This more than brightened our day!

Yet another beautiful milestone we're able to share in our journey together. Always leaning into a positive mindset. A silver-lining indeed!

– Cynthia Perello (Team Perello)

And Then the Fires Came

The election had already made us sick to our stomachs.
It all felt so toxic, infuriating, deflating, paralyzing, depressing.
Some of us took the "eat, drink, and be merry" approach.
Better enjoy every moment we can before January 20th,
when Enters the Dragon "Terrible" *(French pronunciation)*.
So we ate too much, drank too much, smoked too much.
But we needed our friends, gathering, embracing, rejuvenating.
We had just about anesthetized ourselves into amnesia,
and then the fires came . . .
On Tuesday, the Palisades combusted.
A black cloud of, "Now what?" engulfed us.
I didn't even get out of bed on Wednesday,
let the news burn into my brain.
I smoldered with the scenes on the screen.
Finally, I couldn't take it anymore
and escaped into a PBS comfort series.
That worked for a few hours.
Then the phone flared, it was my poet pal, Ricardo.
We usually greet each other as "Love Bug,"
but instead, he sounded serious when he said, "Kennon!"
He tells me Runyon Canyon is ablaze.
I know Runyon is less than a mile from my place
and think I may have to evacuate.
I thank him and switch back to the news.
I haven't combed my hair or brushed my teeth all day.
My first thought is denial; I just don't want to deal.
Besides, where would I go? I don't own a car.
Maybe this is where my fat ass gets roasted.
These thoughts swiftly drift away with the relentless winds.
I could hop the train, but that might be bedlam.
Then my eyes lock on my bike, that's the ticket,

and whatever I can tie to my handlebars.
I get dressed, brush my teeth.
I begin to stuff what very well might become
my last remaining possessions in two nylon bags.
I pack a canvas bag with electronics and shoes.
Ten minutes go by in a hurry-flurry.
The phone blares a searing City Alert, "Go now!"
I text my friend, Maggie, she says I can come to her house.
I cinch the bags to my handlebars,
maneuver my bike into the hall.
Thankfully, a neighbor is there.
He holds the 100-year-old elevator door wide
so I can back in and rock the front wheel up inside
dimensions the same as a mid-century phone booth.
It's a 20-30 minute ride to Maggie's, all downhill.
I sail past the backed-up traffic.
When I arrive, Maggie is packing her car.
She wants to go farther away, get a hotel.
Once in the car we ponder which way to go.
Downtown? No, too close to Altadena,
another apocalypse in progress...
Let's make this fun I say, as we head south
with no definite destination in mind.
We pass houses aglow with Christmas lights.
"Yay," I say, "I miss those drives from childhood
cruising neighborhoods for Christmas displays!"
Maggie looks at me astonished, "You're calm under fire!"
She drives on and takes a call from a friend who tells us,
"The Queen Mary is offering discounts to evacuees."
Done! Long Beach here we come!
We arrive before eight and get in a long check-in line.

We live like royal refugees, a sumptuous breakfast included!
At around $120 each, it's like we scored a mini vacation!
Thank you, Queen Mary!
Runyon was contained quickly.
The evacuation order was lifted in thirteen hours.
I was home by noon the next day.
Smoke clung to the air as I peddled uphill in my flimsy mask.
Once home, evidence of my evacuation panic was clear.
I'd left the iron gate to my apartment ajar and
hadn't even locked the inner apartment door!
I'd left all the lights on, even those on my artificial tree.
It was the third Christmas tree I'd erected since November—
but that's another story for another time.
I was home, I was safe, my apartment hadn't been disturbed.
My neighborhood had been spared. Thank You God!
I was one of the lucky ones, so grateful to still have my home.
We pray, donate, pull together for those less fortunate,
those left with only the clothes on their backs
but still in better shape than the Palestinians.
The conflagration continued and more wildfires erupted.
A friend says, "This feels like 9/11 all over again."
The fires are a warning of dark days ahead.
Enter the Dragon Terrible breathing hellfire and brimstone,
scorching our nation, incinerating our institutions,
enflaming allied relations, gaslighting human rights.
Does anyone else feel like they're in a movie mashup of
Manchurian Candidate and Kazan's *A Face in the Crowd*?
Suddenly the theatre becomes a car in an endless,
slow-motion collision with an oncoming train!
Is this the new normal to return with the winds each year?
Is this the vengeance he promised to all his foes?
Who knows if it was lone crazies or proud boys?

We withdraw in silence, try not to think of arsonists.
The Dragon Terrible chants, "Drill, baby, drill!"
Storms and floods intensify from coast to coast.
Earthquakes emerge and rumble repeatedly.
We hold our breath dreading the next catastrophe.
Be prepared, stand strong, stand free . . .

– Kennon B. Raines

Like a Movie

This time I'm only observer,
appropriator of trauma and disaster.
I can report what I viewed and smelled,
animal instincts shaken awake.
Because this time it wasn't me.

I've been too close before,
heard sheriff bullhorn evacuation
warnings, saw the thin red line like
a hot new incision spread wider and
crest the nearest ridgeline.

This time I could actually
feel the sky darken, smoke lowering,
billowing from mountains over beach and bay
provoking sunsets palled an unnatural orange,
scent of doused campfires.

We're still finding
ash on our balcony miles away from backyard
brush, ignited hillsides; it just keeps drifting,
settling, laying toxic in every crevice, on any
level surface. In all the wildfires

I've been through here
I've never seen so many palm trees burn,
rows of birthday tragedy candles, or
bushy-haired stick men, their hair aflame,
running stiff, screaming into the sea.

Hard for me, in my role
as audience, as non-combatant, to say it:
this time maybe the lucky ones lost
everything. Those homes left unscorched,
solitary or in smoke-damaged minyans,

survivors' guilt in the middle
of blocks—spared Santa Ana furies, ember
cascades, retardant strafes, hyena looters—
are now carrion for remediation vultures.
The questions beg: "Stay?" Go?" "Go where?"

It will take years.

– Jim Natal

Wild winds whipped war
Used fire as a weapon
Neighborhood destroyed

– Mona Jean Cedar

To the Living, Breathing Arsonists, the Molochs of Electricity

Fire is an archaeologist
Falsely accused of plundering
A tomb it only wanted to preserve!
And now, released from prison,
It craves the restitution
It deserves; but first let it devour
The flimsy, mythic evidence
Of guesswork detectives ignoring facts:
The sloppy arson of the Molochs
Of electricity stands self-condemned.
The ravaging to come is not revenge:
Only equilibrium demanding they restore
what they destroyed or surrender everything
they've hoarded. How seething the flames still are!
How charred the prison walls!

– Bill Mohr

Rivers of Debris Quilt the Sand at Low Tide

We don't know what it is, this strange burnt sienna settled along the curves of grandmother's beach at the marina. Dogs leap & run as always. They chase orange balls, skid obliviously through the marvels of washed-up designs beautiful enough for a museum show—a winding flow of rust colored detritus specked with neon candy wrappers, water bottles, beer cans. A child spins cartwheels, legs scissored in the air. She can stand on her hands, face flush with blood as she balances upside down like the Hanged Man. We don't know what these rivers of red are— these unexpected swirly drawings sloughed up by the sea's constant rhythm. There are no swimmers. No lifeguard to ask. One old surfer walks thigh deep hauling his heavy antique board, watches the froth of dirty waves, turns defeated, trudges inland over the long white length of sand. A bulldog runs free, mouth stuffed with a small chunk of scorched wood he has found. He drops it to snuffle the sea lace of clay hued foam. The sand is red. The water is red. The squiggles of patterns slither north & south as if a mythical snake has arrived to slowly feast. Then we understand. We're walking on houses, on phone poles, signage—sycamore & oak. We are walking on the Reel Inn, on hearths & bedding, couches & heirlooms, on books & books of family photos. We are walking on the remains of the burned city washed up on shore. We are walking on lives. The currents of the story go on as far as we can see. You start to weep. We both do.

— **Holaday Mason**

The Arsonist

Why tour fire damage at all when the golf course is over there?

Where does a rapist store his compassion?

Who was embraced? Who was repelled? Who felt empathy and what did it cost?

Who was given a red hat?

How many voter ID requirements does it cost to release emergency funding?

How many felony convictions does it take to withhold aid?

What is the disrespect capacity in Air Force One's wings?

Where do domestic workers go when houses they clean disappear?

Where do domestic workers go when the man with the disaster aid disappears them?

How do you get making America great again out of your lungs?

What is the paperwork turnaround time on restoration of dignity?

Who asks the question "what is hazardous waste?"

What is the toll on your neck muscles when nodding at lies?

How fast does praise turn to ash? What is the expiration date on a promise?

How do you tour fire damage with a political arsonist?

– Jeffrey Bryant

And for California, it's Only June

Ranting about golden hours and temperate climates   and the blonde
she used to be   hot boxing   Salems   her unholy halo of minty smoke.

Just shows up   no call   says her place burned down   and the place
before that.   *The tomorrow woman.*   We once gave each other nicknames.

We were that close.   Now she sits in my captain's chair   a hard glance at me
and I'm listening   looking west   her narrowed eyes   the bracing nerviness

of glacier blue.   Out back   where we felled the willow   mockingbird parents
in the stubbly growth   feed their young   in short bursts of hop   flit   fly

perilously exposed   in the drought-starved yard.   *It's not natural*   she's saying
in her strafed voice   pulling at the pony tail   she can't make right.

Over Zoom her daughters laid it down   they won't bring kids into this world.
Not now   I tried not to scream   as our blood red sun sinks
                    into the maudlin mauve.

— Beth Ruscio

Wildfires, Redux

Bukowski says, "What matters most is how well you walk through the fire." I lived that childhood, grew up in parched canyons, wildfires a threat—no, a promise. When they raged, when the wind whipped spark into frenzy, we could see the tangerine flames of the Bel Air fire from miles away, their deadly, destructive dance a horror film made real. At six I knew the drill: a duffle bag of essentials at the ready, gallons of water in the trunk. Always a full tank of gas. The horror in my six-year-old heart as the flames made their way down the canyon, licking at our lives.

When the Palisades turned inferno, when Altadena burned to a crisp, I was miles away in the Mojave, in no danger, glued to the TV news. Yet somehow, I was in the midst of it, a child again, terrified, clinging to my mother's skirt. Some traumas cannot be cauterized; they flare up at the least provocation.

I know a poet who has that Bukowski quote tattooed large on his right forearm. He says it reminds him to keep his wits about him. To be ready to douse or flee. I tell him some things can't be avoided or excised; a singe, a smear of smoke made soot, a conflagration. The terrors of a lifetime.

– **Alexis Rhone Fancher**

Ashes at Random

Ashes, ashes falling softly from the sky
like blankets of fine black snow
no two flakes alike

Randomly sifting through window screens
clogging my nostrils
coating my countertops

What charred memories, these
whose cherished rooftops, paint brushes, guitars
priceless heirlooms, favorite chairs

Simple enough for me
to wipe my sinks clean, but
Oh! The tragedies these ashes signify

As they're falling, families huddle
unprotected from relentless flames
holding up in hotels if they're lucky

shelters and tents small comfort
compared to the tremendous loss
of home and hearth

Not dozens suffering, not hundreds
but thousands of evacuees, all beyond shocked
all frantically wondering what their futures may hold

Simple enough for me
to type these lines, But
Oh! How I feel for those displaced

Refugees to the whims of nature
Refugees through no known fault
Random victims of assault

– jerry the priest

Antidote for a Firestorm

A firecracker began it,
A series of pretty lights in the sky
That quickly festooned the city
With unwanted flames.

The famed searchlights of Hollywood
Became the heated fangs of a
Mega monster
That devoured, with no preference
Delicious homes of the rich
And crumbling dwellings of the poor.

The unseasonable
Warm breezes of an eccentric winter
Fed the fires
That multiplied with demon party abandon.

Kindled also were the tempers
Of the natives who fought
With each other over who was to blame
While the self-defined King laughed
Derisively and pretended to play a fiddle.

In the midst of the vermillion hell
Stood a child holding
An angel food cake.
Food for the fire fighters
Or an offering to the
Angry fire gods.
Either way, she hoped
To douse the flames
Of humankind's worst
Mistakes
With someone's
Kind intentions.

– Lynne Bronstein

I Know Too Well
after the Palisades fire

Summer used to laugh at me
I never brushed my hair
Stacking stones on the beach

Oftentimes I bothered
The ocean
Which isn't all that difficult

Today I fear the arrival of winter
Its importunate snout already
Sniffing out fields of dry sagebrush

I detest the memory of you disheveled
On a sand drift
Where I found you once unwanted

So many long nights remembered
(tant de longues nuits!)
And our odd old stories of the setting sun

I insist on reinventing them
Though these days I'm reluctant to
Make you laugh while lighting a candle

While nursing a small flame
(The fires almost took our house)
Nodding a small nod

To those calamities
Every one of us
Knows so well conflagrations

Of grief and heartbreak
Swell the rising tide the rolling
Swell on which I'm riding

Into another season of undoing
Of bad luck bad omens
Faux pas last straws *adieus*

    And yet our Topanga house
    Still stands
    With its wooden frame its

    Bleached clapboard siding
    That smells of smoke
    That won't last another twenty

    Years of epic drought
    There is no phoenix here
    In these scorched mountains

    No rising up and eating
    Men like air

– Gail Wronsky

listening to your playlist while driving made me feel like i was in your car again going around l.a.

—driving the 5, thinking of damian
    for no reason at all—i hold his surrender
        inside the back pocket of my iris

    ways he hurt himself to bury a deadname
            dark sleepy eye acquiesce shapeshifter

—i miss the color of his grogginess—

        taiwanese night market rummaging for his
        mother's shadow in dizzy streets of burgundy
        bone broth warm salt & ash tucked in no light

i'd reach for the fishbone stuck in his throat

                if he'd let me

driving the 5, i scream—
    suffocate my goddamn self
    past griffith park thinking of damian
        for no reason at all—i hold his smile
            inside the trunk of my under-the-influence
                self-aware pity, mirrorless gaze haunts me

i wonder if i ever gave damian enough of my love

            —my love, i hope you're okay in the bay
        i hope you don't stumble around searching
            for your keys in the morning
        for no reason at all—i suffocate myself
        only to recall october sunset embers

        fire burnt mid-city late drives & swallowing
           ash—probably could've died if i made
that right lane switch   heard your voice instead

i've been trying to find you inside a merwin poem

            a later piece without punctuation

  & it's the saddest ones who have the raspiest voices—
why'd you leave me in a city that is constantly burning

—driving the 5, whispering to myself
   who's judas in all of this, thinking of damian
     for no reason at all—i stroke my lament till
        it becomes prayer or sacrilege fragment

            are some of the old colors still there

  i've been searching for you between quintessence & dusk

      have you finally collected your teeth

- jimmy vega

The Renter Key

In my front left pocket is a key. I pat my thigh and can feel it. It's on a ring alongside a metal tag with a few numbers, the ring on a clip with a few others: a key to our house, fob keys for our cars, the key to the house I grew up in, even though Mom died 12 years ago and we sold the place a few years later.

That other key, the one with the tag, has been in my pocket for years, for decades now, unused. It fits a lock on a metal box clear across town, up in the hills. It's a safe deposit box gotten at the Bank of America in Altadena, on upper Lake, from where on a clear day you can see all the way to Catalina.

"What's in it?" Susan has asked me when I've mentioned it over the last few years.

"I really don't remember," I've answered. "Maybe some jewelry. Maybe some papers. I'm not sure."

There is one thing I do know was put in the box, I told her: a VHS tape. On it is a tour around a house, not far from that bank branch. Furniture, art, shelves of books, of records, of CDs, various other items. That's what was documented. Just in case, you know?

Here and there on the map on the screen were little black triangles and little red triangles, sparsely populating patches of gray. Black meant yes, still there. Red meant no, gone. The gray patches, don't know yet.

One night in the mid-1990s, I stood on the roof, hose in hand, wetting down everything I could—the shingles, the trees.

Below me, in the carport, our cars were packed. Documents, photo albums, a few pieces of art. A friend had come to help.

A little later I walked to the end of the block, looked up the cross street to the hills which were aglow, flames leaping here and there. The fire covered the slopes, about half a mile away. But there was no way it could come down all the way here, right? Too much for it to get through. The winds weren't strong. But . . . we didn't know. We just didn't know. Turned out we were right. I didn't get there. We were safe . . . but . . .

That's why we made that tape, just in case. Proof it was there. Insurance, all that. Just in case, you know?

More black triangles. Even more red triangles. Less gray. But still don't know.

One marriage came to an end in that house. Another took root there. There was a cat named Zelda, a dog named Molly, a parakeet named Man Ray, a bunny named Lucy. When Zelda died there was Zeke. When Molly died there was Hayley, and then also Bix.

There were parties and dinners and music and even some dancing.

There were the friends who lived in the makeshift converted garage apartment for a while.

There was coming home late one night from a concert I was covering to be told that my dad had died. There was the next morning when somehow, some way, I sat at my over-cluttered desk in my rat-pack office and wrote my piece before driving up to Santa Barbara to be with mom and my family.

And there was cancer, and chemo, and radiation, and, for a while, remission.

There were trips planned, trips packed for, trips launched, all over the world.

Refreshing the page makes more triangles, like ants swarming. Or soldiers attacking. Refresh again a few hours later, even more triangles. Some isolated. Some in clusters. Refresh the next morning, more. More clusters. Less gray space.

I zoom in to one part. More street names come on. Lake, then west to Fair Oaks, further west to Lincoln. Altadena Drive, then north a few blocks to Loma Alta. There's Chaney Trail, There's Olive, the place we'd rented. What was the number? How far up the street?

Then Laurel. Two blocks long, that's all. A gray patch. Still gray. Still unknown. But above it mostly red, more red with each refresh of the page, it seemed. Now closer. Below it a mix of red, black and gray, filling in. East and west, the same.

It feels . . . strangely distant. Why strangely, I have to wonder? It's been 24 years since we moved away, sold that house, packed everything up, junked everything we didn't want to pack. That old Sears Silvertone Twin Twelve guitar amp that I bought for 50 bucks from a college friend? The head, with that reverb coil that would go *sproing* if you just slightly bumped it, made it. But the cabinet, beat-up gray with those two foot-wide speakers? Went missing. Never to be seen again. Some of the movers were musicians . . . but . . . I just don't want to think like that.

First there's a letter. Then an email. Then another letter. More emails. The bank was damaged, the boxes moved, secured in a new location. We will give updates soon, they say. Another letter and email. They're all accounted for, but no telling what state the contents might be in. Heat, smoke, ash. Please contact us to make arrangements.

All these years of not knowing. All these years of wondering. All these years of, really, not thinking about it much except every January when the notice came about the box rental fee being charged.

Didn't I want to know? Susan would ask. Sure. I did. But it was a long drive from Santa Monica.

This year the notice came just a few days before the fires broke out. And yet I didn't even think of the bank as we looked at the photos and videos, read and heard reports, many from friends, some from family. Hadn't even thought of how the house on Laurel Drive might have fared until a few days after the fires. It just didn't come to mind. Then, at some point, that OH! moment. Oh!

Then the map with its gray, its red, its black.

And then what had been gray, the place of the house, the place I had lived, a place of my life . . . now red.

Are you nervous? Susan asks as we drive to the appointment we've made.

Nervous?

About what might be in it?

No, not nervous, I say. But maybe I am. A little.

I pat my thigh and feel the key.

– Steve Hochman

Pagamento

I beg fire   burn away indifference –
Set ablaze   bigotry

    spare school buildings & nests
    torch   poverty & greed

In your hot fury I send a mother's tears
to rise an eagle with elk & wolves in its wings

set free protection   let the blaze change
its diet, may flames crave
demon whispers in otherworlds, instead

Earth Mother

    together   we offer
    this pagamento.

    Plant fresh seeds
    where families cry

    where the already burned
    by virtue of surviving, reside

    Refuse fire's blind fury
    poets meet you in the ashes
    poets tumble into scorching tears
    tread grief with you

Together   we rebuild

what's left ancestor rings in a safe
         a young mother's Tree of Life statue
         below hardened soot may we find emerald
         regrowth green, possibility

Earth Mother

   from our soul pockets
   hear our apologies

   Pagamentos. Payments
   for the wreckage, rapes
   stoked by his systems
   already burning us away.

   Send the rain, soothe & cleanse
   sadness & confusion, in collective weeping

   may rebirths dance   may new poems grow
   new wildnerness new homes new communities

   may meaning & abundance restore –

Earth Mother

   with this pagamento
   I turn counter-clockwise
   three times

taste cocoa in my throat
holy wood spreads
through my lungs & nose

Earth Mother

may wildfire
feel a full belly
& go away –

– K.R. Morrison

Perello Family's Journey to Re-Establish Our Lives
Go Fund Me, July 25, 2025

Losing our home in the Eaton fires this past January was more than heartbreaking. It felt like watching years of memories, sentimental items which held so much significance in my life, such as my wedding dress, other important milestones, I love, go up in smoke. And yet, somehow, even in the middle of all that loss, I've found pieces of joy, moments of peace, and quiet sources of comfort that I hold onto tightly.

JOY & PEACE

What brings me joy now isn't big or flashy—it's the little things. The sound of my only remaining sister's laughter when we remember something from childhood. Dining, watching movies, laughter and poignant heart felt discussions with my in-laws and close friends. Or mottos my mama used to say to us to help developers and support our journey. A warm cup of coffee in the morning, even if it's not in the kitchen I once knew.

Morning breathing meditations, gratified sessions with my husband, praying for ourselves and those we love in hopes that life will be more clear and the journey more bearable. A sincere and transparent and supportive handwritten note or a friend we hadn't heard from in years. These things remind me that love isn't tied to a house—it travels with you.

Peace finds me in unexpected places. Sometimes I park in front of our property, and I walk throughout the property. Sometimes I close my eyes, picturing positive memories in the very spot that I walk/stand. Even with the scars the fire left behind, I watch the earth slowly healing. I see flowers blooming where ash once settled, and I remember that life finds a way.

The mountains still stand, and so do we.

We love and adore you. Thank you for your continued support.

– Team Perello

WE WILL REBUILD

I GAZED IN DISBELIEF AT SUCH A HORRIFIC SIGHT
AS FIRES BLAZED IN THOSE WINDY L.A. NITES
AS WE CHOKED FROM THE BILLOWING SMOKE
WE WATCHED AS HOMES BURNED TO THE GROUND
SOME LIVES WERE LOST SOME WERE THANKFULLY FOUND
THIS IS NO HOLLYWOOD SCENE ON THE SCREEN
THIS IS HARSH REALITY MANY FORCED BY EVACUATIONS
TO SECURE SHELTER AMID THIS DEVASTATION
AS WE ALL COME TOGETHER TO DO WHAT WE CAN
BELIEVE IN DUE TIME WE'LL BE BACK ON OUR FEET ONCE AGAIN

WE WILL REBUILD
WE WILL RISE FROM THE ASHES AND SOAR ONCE MORE
WE WILL BUILD BETTER THAN BEFORE

WE GIVE THANKS FOR THE FIRST RESPONDERS
THOSE WHO PUT THEIR OWN LIVES AT RISK
AND GRATEFUL FOR THE DONATIONS
THAT ARE SORELY NEEDED TO ASSIST
THOSE WHO HAVE LOST SO MUCH
THINGS THAT CAN NEVER BE REPLACED
IT WON'T BE EASY TO REBUILD
THERE WILL BE MANY CHALLENGES TO FACE
BUT AS LONG AS WE ALL PULL TOGETHER
WE CAN BUILD THIS CITY BETTER THAN EVER

THE WINGS OF THE CITY OF ANGELS HAVE BEEN BURNED
BUT WE REFUSE TO BE GROUNDED
WE WILL FLY HIGH AGAIN CUZ WE ARE SURROUNDED
BY AN ENERGY THAT SAYS NO MATTER HOW ROUGH OR
    HOW LONG
WE WILL SUCCEED CUZ WE ARE L.A. STRONG
WE'RE IN A STATE OF DEVASTATION WARNINGS OF
    EVACUATION
WE'LL OVERCOME THIS SITUATION WE WILL NOT FAIL
WE WILL PREVAIL

– **La Rombé** ♪

About the Contributors

Susan Auerbach is a retired professor of education from Altadena, CA, who returned in midlife to her first love of creative writing. In addition to her chapbook, *In the Mourning Grove* (Finishing Line Press, 2024), her poems have appeared in *Rattle, Spillway, Gyroscope Review,* and other journals, as well as in her memoir, *I'll Write Your Name on Every Beach: A Mother's Quest for Comfort, Courage & Clarity After Suicide Loss* (Jessica Kingsley Publishers, 2017).

Until January 7, 2025, **Lin Nelson Benedek** and her husband, Tom, lived in Altadena under the spell of orange blossoms and the San Gabriel Mountains. They currently reside in Playa Vista. A longtime psychotherapist, Lin is passionate about the importance of human connection and believes in the power of poetry to heal, connect and enchant us. Her poems have been published in numerous journals, in seven anthologies and in four full-length collections published by Kelsay Books.

Mary Anne Berry is a retired high school teacher of French and English. Her love affair with poetry began in early childhood, and she is never happier than in a group of like-minded poets working to hone their craft. She hosts a group monthly at her home in Pasadena, California.

Michelle Bitting was recently named a City of L.A. Department of Cultural Affairs Individual Artist Grantee and is the author of six poetry collections, including *Nightmares & Miracles* (*Two Sylvias Press*, 2022), winner of the Wilder Prize and named one of *Kirkus Reviews* 2022 Best of Indie. Her chapbook *Dummy Ventriloquist* was published in 2024 by *C & R Press*. Recent poetry appears on *The Slowdown, Thrush, Cleaver, The Poetry Society of New York's Milk Press, Heavy Feather Review, Split Lip, National Poetry Review, SWWIM, ONE ART,* and is featured as

Poem of the Week in *The Missouri Review*. Her forthcoming collection *Ruined Beauty* will be published by *Walton Well Press* in Fall, 2025. Bitting is writing a novel that centers around Los Angeles and her great grandmother, stage and screen actor Beryl Mercer, and is Senior Lecturer in Creative Writing and Literature at Loyola Marymount University.

Laurel Ann Bogen has returned to the page after a several years' long silence. She is the author of eleven books of poetry and short fiction, the most recent, *Psychosis in the Produce Department*, was published by Red Hen Press.

Lynne Bronstein is the author of *Nasty Girls* (Four Feathers Press) and four other books of poetry. She has been published in magazines ranging from *Playgirl* to *Chiron Review*, from *Lummox* to anthologies in England, Ireland, Canada, and India. Her short fiction has appeared in magazines and anthologies and has been read on National Public Radio. She also writes a column on Facebook and Substack called *Show Biz Cats*.

Jeffrey Bryant is a Pushcart nominated queer poet from Los Angeles. His work has appeared in the *LA Weekly*, *LA Times*, *Poetic Diversity*, *New Verse News*, *Poetrysuperhighway.com*, *Synkroniciti*, *Quill and Echo*, *Tension Literary*, *Journal of the Plague Years*, *Coiled Serpent*, *Altadena Literary Review*, *Shadowplay* and *Sparring with Beatnik Ghosts*. He is a featured poet in the forthcoming spring edition of *Cholla Needles Literary Journal*. His debut collection *The Catacombs of Vanished Lovers* was released in the summer of 2025 on Cherry Pie Press. You can find him on Instagram @jeffreybryant88.

Mona Jean Cedar has been spilling her spoken word poetry with American Sign Language (ASL) around the globe for over 30 years. Her poetry pedigree includes being on the Long Beach Slam team; interpreted for the National Slams and the Women of the World Slams until they imploded; interpreting for the Coupe du Monde de Poesie (an international slam) in Paris for five years when in the final year she actually competed and represented the USA, multitudinous readings, a few Dada events… presently performs with her husband, a circuit bender (google it). A bunch of other stuff too… has a dance company choreographing with international signs… Burning Man, … blah blah blah.

Teresa Mei Chuc was born in Sài Gòn, Vietnam shortly after the Vietnam War and grew up in Pasadena and Altadena, California. Altadena Poet Laureate, Editor-in-Chief (2018-2020) and Pasadena Rose Poet since 2016, Teresa Mei Chuc is the author of three books of poetry, *Invisible Light* (Many Voices Press, 2018), *Keeper of the Winds* (FootHills Publishing, 2014) and *Red Thread* (Fithian Press, 2012). Her recent poetry chapbook, *Incidental Takes*, was published by Hummingbird Press in 2023. Teresa is a public school English teacher in Los Angeles in her twentieth-year teaching.

Jeanette Clough holds an M.A. from the University of Chicago, Division of the Humanities, and was employed as an art librarian at the Getty Research Institute. She has edited for *Solo, A Journal of Poetry*, reviewed for *Poetry International,* and was Artist in Residence at Joshua Tree National Park. Her current poetry collection, *Fire Roulette* (Cahuenga Press, 2025), features lyrical and narrative poems of personal risk.

Brendan Constantine is a poet based in Los Angeles. His work has appeared in *Poetry, The Nation, Best American Poetry, Tin House, Ploughshares,* and *Poem-a-Day* among other journals. A popular performer, Brendan Constantine has presented his work to audiences throughout the U.S. and Europe, also appearing on NPR's All Things Considered, TED ED, numerous podcasts, and YouTube. He currently teaches at the Windward School and the Los Angeles County Museum of Art. His fifth collection, *The Opposites Game* is forthcoming from Red Hen Press.

Iris De Anda is a Guanaca Tapatia poet and musician who has been featured with Pacifica Radio, organized with Academy of American Poets, performed at LA Latino Book Festival, UNAM in CDMX, Casa de las Americas in Havana, Cuba and is named one of Today's Revolutionary Women of Color. Author of *Codeswitch: Fires from Mi Corazon* 2014 Los Writers Underground Press, *Roots of Redemption: You have No Right to Remain Silent* 2022 Flowersong Press, and *Loose Poems* a collection of B-side poems and songs 2022 Multimedia Militia. www.lawriterunderground.com

Alexis Rhone Fancher is a poet and photographer. She has published ten books of poetry, most recently *Erotic: New & Selected*, *Brazen* (both NYQ Books), and *Triggered* (MacQ Press). Her photo book of 100+ Southern California poets will be published in early 2026 by Moon Tide Press. A multiple Best of the Net and Pushcart Prize nominee, Alexis just won Best Micro Fiction, 2025. She lives in the Mojave Desert. www.alexisrhonefancher.com

Pushcart-nominated poet **Rich Ferguson** has shared the stage with Patti Smith, Wanda Coleman, Moby, and other esteemed artists. He is a featured performer in the film *What About Me?* featuring Michael Stipe, k.d. lang, and others. His poetry has been widely published, and his spoken word videos have appeared in international film festivals. Ferguson's third poetry collection, *Somewhere, a Playground*, was released by Moon Tide Press in October of 2025.

Kathleen Florence is a writer and director whose work spans screen, stage, and page. Her work has been published in multiple journals and anthologies, including L.A.'s *Cultural Daily*, *Paris Lit Up*, and *Maintenant* issues 10 - 19 (Three Rooms Press). Her poetry collection *Prayers with a Side of Cash* was published by Moon Tide Press in 2025.

Land Flowers is a Jamaican-American poet, novelist and essayist based in Los Angeles, California. His poetry has been featured in publications such as *The Sparring Artists: Anthology of Sparring with Beatnik Ghosts #2*. He briefly attended Santa Monica College where he studied philosophy. His debut poetry collection is set to arrive in winter of 2026.

Kat Georges is an author, poet, playwright, and graphic designer. Her most recent book is the poetry collection, *Awe and Other Words Like Wow*. She is co-editor of the annual contemporary dada journal, *Maintenant*. Her poems have recently appeared in *NYC from the Inside, Arriving at a Shoreline, Mas Tequila,* and many more. She lives in New York City and is co-director of Three Rooms Press.

S.A. Griffin lives, loves, and works in Los Angeles. He has been publishing books, chapbooks, broadsides and recordings on his Rose of Sharon imprint since 1988.

Spencer L. Griffin has been a guitarist for 25 years and a music lover all his life. He enjoys spending time with his cat, Clarence, and his girlfriend, Mackenzie, and is a proud member of the all-neurodivergent rock quintet, Neurotribe. His collection of children's poetry, *Poem Pie* (Rose of Sharon) debuted in 2024 to universal praise.

Susan Hayden is author of the hybrid memoir; *Now You Are a Missing Person* (Moon Tide Press). It was a Kirkus Reviews' Best Indie Book of 2024, after receiving the Kirkus Star. She's been published in numerous anthologies, including *From Venice to Venice: Poets of California and Italy* (El Martillo Press), *Beat Not Beat* (Moon Tide Press) and *The Black Body* (Seven Stories Press). She is Creator/Producer of Library Girl, now in its 17th year.

Steve Hochman has covered music for 40 years, most prominently with the *Los Angeles Times, Rolling Stone*, KPCC and KQED. Currently he's a featured writer in *SPIN*, New Orleans' *OffBeat* and *The Bluegrass Situation*, and serves as a frequent moderator of events at the Grammy Museum. In recent years, with the loving encouragement of his wife, Susan Hayden, he has also embraced a more personal voice, writing pieces for her monthly live literary series, Library Girl.

jerry the priest, legal name Jerome Dunn, has been creating material for exhibition, publication and live presentation since 1979, when he studied experimental music at the University of Redlands. A vocal performer since early childhood, his formal study of music began with his first trombone lesson in 1967. He holds a BA in Performance Studies from Naropa University, and an MFA in Theater Directing/Production from California Institute of the Arts. His latest collection of poetry and prose, *Brute Entropy*, is available on amazon.com, and wherever he performs.

La Rombé is a Grammy honored singer, songwriter and producer from Philadelphia. After some local success in Philadelphia, he relocated to L.A. where he was signed to Curtis Mayfield's Curtom label. He currently runs his own LoveLyte Productions. With TV/film credits, LoveLyte also works with various artists, most notably multi-Grammy winner Keb Mo, which led to honors for a co/write on the album. His latest project was *We Will Rebuild*, a song dedicated to the city after the fires.

Tom Laichas is author of three books of poetry, most recently *Three Hundred Streets of Venice California* (FutureCycle Press, 2023). His work has appeared or is forthcoming in *Prairie Schooner, Plume, The Los Angeles Times, The Irish Times, Blue Unicorn* and elsewhere. The featured American poet at the *High Window Review* (UK), his work has also won awards from *Jabberwock Review, Puerto del Sol*, and *Prime 53*. He lives with his family in Venice, California.

Los Angeles poet **Rick Lupert** created Poetry Super Highway (poetrysuperhighway.com) and hosted the Cobalt Cafe weekly reading for almost 21 years, which has lived on as a Zoom series since 2020. He's authored 28 collections of poetry, most recently *It's Spritz O'Clock Somewhere* and *God Wrestler: a Poem for Every Torah Portion* and edited the anthologies *A Poet's Siddur, Ekphrastia Gone Wild, A Poet's Haggadah*, and *The Night Goes on All Night*. He writes a Jewish Poetry column for www.JewishJournal.com, and the daily web comic *Cat and Banana* with Brendan Constantine. He reads his poetry wherever they let him.

Suzanne Lummis' fourth collection, *Crime Wave* was published by Giant Claw, imprint of What Books, in Fall 2025—also that year, her anthology, national in scope, *Poetry Goes to the Movies* (Pacific Coast Poetry Series), the first such exploration to rise from L.A. Her poems have appeared in *Plume, Ploughshares, Catamaran, Rattle, The New Yorker.* She was a 2018/19 City of Los Angeles (COLA) fellow, and with that endowment produced the provocative *Tweets from Hell.*

Phoebe MacAdams was born and raised in New York City but has mostly lived in California. She moved to L.A. in 1986. With the poets James Cushing, the late Holly Prado and Harry Northup, she is a founding member of Cahuenga Press, which now includes the poet Jeanette Clough. She taught English at Roosevelt High School in Boyle Heights until her retirement in 2011. She has published seven books of poetry, the last five with Cahuenga Press, including in 2016, her new and selected volume, *The Large Economy of the Beautiful.* In 2017, Beyond Baroque published *Every Bird Helps: A Cancer Journal.* She lives in Pasadena with her husband, Ron Ozuna.

Sarah Maclay's fourth chapbook, *The H.D. Sequence—A Concordance,* and *Nightfall Marginalia,* a 2023 Foreword INDIES Finalist for Poetry, her fifth full-length collection, follow a Yaddo residency, a COLA Individual Artist Fellowship, the *Tampa Review* Prize for Poetry and a Pushcart Special Mention, and publications in *APR, FIELD, Ploughshares, The Writer's Chronicle, The Best American Erotic Poems, Poetry International,* where she served as Book Review Editor, and elsewhere. She currently hosts Poetry.LA's *The Poetry of Night.*

kamla maya, *Malibu, Macramé & Mangione. To Live & Die in L.A.* Been writing diary entries since the '70s. Journals, monologues, poems, song lyrics. L.A. native and advocate. Stunned and horrified at what Los Angeles has become. Fighting so hard to get local governments to care about us and amend terrible decisions. Ignored and overlooked. My three sentences in this book float in my head all the time and have more power than my other actions.

Holaday Mason's sixth full length collection of poetry, *As If Scattered* was published by Giant Claw/What Books Press in 2024—other collections include, *Towards the Forest, Dissolve, The Red Bowl: A Fable in Poems, The "She" Series: A Venice Correspondence* (with Sarah Maclay), *The Weaver's Body.* Her work has appeared in *Hotel Amerika, Spillway, Solo, Pool, Poetry International, The Laurel Review* and more. Co-editor for Beyond Baroque's *Echo 68.* Currently poetry editor for *Furious Pure,* Ms. Mason is also a fine art photographer focusing on the surrealism within nature and the beauty of humans as a part of nature. www.holadaymason.com

Ellyn Maybe, a Southern California based poet, United States Artist nominee, is the author of numerous books, and is widely anthologized. She also has two highly acclaimed poetry/music albums, *Rodeo for the Sheepish* (Hen House Studios) and *Skywriting with Glitter* (ellyn & robbie). Ellyn Maybe & PJ Swift, aka Word Troubadours are collaborating on a poetry book to be released in 2025 (Mystic Boxing Commission).

While a resident of New York City **Richard Modiano** became active in the literary community connected to the Poetry Project where he came to know Gregory Corso, Allen Ginsberg, Anne Waldman, William S. Burroughs and Ted Berrigan. In 2001 he was a programmer at Beyond Baroque Literary/Arts Center, joined the Board of Trustees in 2006, and from 2010 to 2019, he served as Executive Director. The Huffington Post named him as one of 200 people doing the most to promote poetry in the United States. Richard Modiano is the winner of the 2022 Joe Hill Prize for labor poetry and is a Pushcart Prize nominee. His collection *The Forbidden Lunchbox* is published by Punk Hostage Press.

Bill Mohr has worked as an editor, publisher, literary historian, and poet since the early 1970s. His books include *Holdouts: The Los Angeles Poetry Renaissance 1948-1992* (University of Iowa Press; 2011) and a bilingual edition of poems, *Pruebas Ocultas* (Bonobos Editores, Mexico; 2015). What Books will publish *Remiges: Collected Longer Poems* in the fall of 2026. www.koanship.com

Chris Morris has written books about Bob Dylan and Los Lobos. His work has also appeared in John Doe and Tom DeSavia's *Under the Big Black Sun* and *More Fun in the New World* and Don Snowden and Gary Leonard's *Make the Music Go Bang!* He co-produced and annotated the 2025 boxed set *The Blasters: An American Music Story*. Like Frankenstein's monster, he is easily scared by fire.

K.R. Morrison is a San Francisco poet who splits her time between the Bay Area and Southern California. She is a three-time Pushcart nominee. Her first collection *Cauldrons* is available from Paper Press Books.

Majid Naficy, the Arthur Rimbaud of Persian poetry, fled Iran in 1983, a year and a half after the execution of his wife, Ezzat in Tehran. Since 1984 Majid has been living in West Los Angeles. He has published five collections of poetry in English including, *Muddy Shoes* (Beyond Baroque, Books, 1999) and *Father and Son* (Red Hen Press, 2003) as well as his doctoral dissertation at UCLA *Modernism and Ideology in Persian Literature: A Return to Nature in the Poetry of Nima Yushij* (University Press of America, 1997). Majid has also published more than twenty books of poetry and essays in Persian. His son, Azad is a singer and songwriter.

Los Angeles poet and literary presenter **Jim Natal** is the author of five full-length poetry books including *Spare Room: Haibun Variations* and *Memory and Rain* as well as the chapbook *Étude in the Form of a Crow*. A new collection, *Everything Changes Everything*, is forthcoming in 2026. His work has appeared widely in journals and anthologies.

Harry E. Northup has had twelve books of poetry published, the latest being: *Love Poem to MPTF* (Cahuenga Press, 2020). He received his B.A. in English from C.S.U.N., where he studied verse with Ann Stanford. Northup made a living as an actor for thirty-four years, acting in thirty-seven films, including *Mean Streets, Taxi Driver, The Silence of the Lambs*; he starred in the acclaimed cult film, *Over the Edge*. He lives in the Motion Picture Country Home in Woodland Hills, California. Harry produces and hosts a weekly, one-hour poetry show on Zoom, *Harry's Poetry Hour, Creative Chaos* MPTF.

I'm **Cynthia Perello**, a Master Certified Coach who has spent many years leading and guiding leaders in corporate America to grow with clarity and purpose. Beyond my professional path, I hold close the roles that define me most deeply: devoted wife, daughter, sister, friend and creative soul. I find immense joy in being of service—and paying it forward. I also find joy in designing wearable art, writing poetry, aqua aerobics, salsa dancing and sharing life with our sweet dog, Gracie. This year, my husband and I celebrate 32 years of marriage—a testament to love, resilience, and the gratitude that carries us through life's seasons.

Puma Perl is a poet, writer, and performer and the author of two chapbooks, and three full-length poetry collections, *knuckle tattoos, Retrograde* (great weather for MEDIA), and *Birthdays Before and After (*Beyond Baroque Books). She is the front woman and primary lyricist in The Puma Perl Band, which brings spoken word together with rock and roll. She's received five awards from the New York Press Association in recognition of her journalism and was the recipient of the 2016 Acker Award in the category of writing. With musician Joe Sztabnik, she recently released a record album, *Under Tenement Skies*, available in vinyl, CD and digital download.

Kennon B. Raines began performing her poetry in NYC nightclubs during the mid '80s. Her YouTube channel, *Kennon B. Raines Poet*, features many recordings of her performances around the East Village, at NYC's Pyramid Club, and various venues after her move to LA. She has performed her poetry in London, Paris, Toronto, Montreal, Boston, Atlanta, Dallas, and San Francisco. Raines has been published in numerous anthologies. In an upcoming project, she and Dr. Mongo Taribubu will be featured in a combined collection to be published by the Mystic Boxing Commission. The book will feature QR codes linking to performances of many of the poems presented in the collection.

Nicca Ray is the author of the memoir *Ray by Ray: A Daughter's Take on the Legend of Nicholas Ray* (Three Rooms Press) and the forthcoming memoir, *Love and Cigarettes* (Punk Hostage Press). She has published three poetry collections, *Go-Go-Go Girl* (Poison Fang Books), *Curve* (Gutter Snob Books), and *Back Seat Baby* (Poison Fang Books). She's an Acker Award recipient for memoir and a Pushcart Prize nominee.

Riot Renwick is a High School student with a deep love for the arts. He loves to spend time in the outdoors and makes nature a common theme in his poetry. He is affiliated with a scouting troop in La Cañada. Seeing friends evacuate with increasing amounts of homes and habitat lost to the fires was a major inspiration for his poem.

Marilyn N. Robertson is a poet from Northeast L.A. Her work has appeared in a number of literary journals, including *Miramar, Salt I* and *II* and *Askew*. She has a poem and essay in the book, *Master Class: The Poetry Mystique*. Two of her poems appear in *Wide Awake, the Poets of Los Angeles and in Pratik, a magazine of Contemporary Writing, Vol. XVIII, No.4,* and *Poetry Goes to the Movies,* all edited by Suzanne Lummis. Her chapbook, *Noir Librarian* is available on Amazon.

Beth Ruscio, whose first paying job was detasseling corn, is the daughter of actors, a poet, and an actor, accomplished and award winning in both fields. Some of those honors in acting: Drama Critics Circle Award, 5 Dramalogue Awards, Best Actress Method Fest; and in poetry: winner of the Brick Road Poetry Prize for *Speaking Parts* (2020), finalist honors for Sunken Garden Poetry Prize, Tupelo Quarterly Prize, Wilder Prize, Two Sylvias Prize. Her essay *In praise of humble ingredients, exalted,* appears in the book, *Outlaw Theatre* (Padua Playwrights Press, 2022), and her poems in these 2025 anthologies: *Poetry Goes to the Movies* (Pacific Coast Poetry Series); *Women in a Golden State* (Gunpowder Press); and forthcoming, *A Picture Is Worth a Poet's Words* (Moon Tide

Press). She shares her life with gifted playwright and teacher Leon Martell and their talented dog, Lolita.

Cathie Sandstrom's poems are online at the Academy of American Poets (poets.org) and have been published in *The Southern Review, Ploughshares, Lyric, Ekphrasis* and other leading literary journals. Anthologies include *Coiled Serpent* and *Wide Awake*. A children's story appeared in *Zizzle*. Of two nominations for a Pushcart prize, one was from *The Southern Review*. Her poem *You, Again* is in the artists' book collection at the Getty Museum, L.A. and at USC. An essay *Braiding the Dreamscape* was published online by the C.G. Jung Society of St. Louis. Her essay *Getting Broken* appears in *Master Class: The Poetry Mystique* by Suzanne Lummis. She writes for the National Veterans Foundation.

Dan Saucedo earned his MFA in Creative Writing from UC Irvine. His work has appeared in *The Napa Review, Thunder in Another City*, and *Writing for Life*. In addition to being a Membership Coordinator at Beyond Baroque, he has served on the executive boards of The California Poetry Society and The California Federation of Chaparral Poets. A retired teacher from the Los Angeles Unified School District, he taught adults who went back to school to earn their high school diplomas. He was honored with an Eddy Award from the LAX Coastal Chamber for Teacher of the Year and an Outstanding Poet award from the Santa Barabara Writer's Conference. He lives a quiet life with his wife Juanita in Venice, California.

Maryrose Smyth's work appears in *Amethyst Review*, June 2022, *Wax Seal Online Literary Magazine*, August 2018, *Mutha Magazine Online*, June 2023 and the anthologies *F.R.&D.*, 2015 and *The Best of the Poetry Salon 2013-2018*. Maryrose received honorable mention in *Jack Grapes' Cultural Weekly Poetry Contest*, 2015 and studies with poet Suzanne Lummis. Maryrose is happy to report she and her family will rebuild paradise take two in their canyon foothills woods in Altadena. Find Maryrose's art at www.studiosmyth.com

3rd-generation Angeleno **Mike Sonksen**, aka Mike the PoeT, is a poet, professor, journalist, historian and tour guide with work in publications like the *Academy of American Poets, Alta, PBS So Cal, Poetry Foundation* and *Westways*. Sonksen's hosted events at Grand Performances and Getty Center. His latest book, *Letters to My City* is published by Writ Large Press.

In a few words, **A.K. Toney** is a griot, musician, and educator. Toney is writing his first book along with a double-album chronicling his life as an ethnographer through the experiences of urban griot. As the Neo Griot, Toney uses musical accompaniment with poetry to provide call and response with listeners as a tool of engagement for participation. He is a founder and the Literacy Coordinator of Reading Is Poetry, LLC. readingispoetry.com. A.K. is also a jazz artist that has worked with Jimetta Rose, Georgia Ann Muldrow, Ryan Porter, Tatiana Tate, Allakoi Peete, Josef Leimberg, and Jamael Dean. aktoney.com aktoney.bandcamp.com

David L. Ulin is the author or editor of twenty books, including the novel *Thirteen Question Method* and *Sidewalking: Coming to Terms with Los Angeles*, shortlisted for the PEN/Diamonstein-Spielvogel Award for the Art of the Essay. The recipient of fellowships from the Guggenheim Foundation, the Lannan Foundation, and Ucross Foundation, as well as a COLA Individual Master Artist Grant from the City of Los Angeles, he is a Professor of English at the University of Southern California, where he co-directs the Los Angeles Institute for the Humanities and edits the journal *Air/Light*.

jimmy vega is the child of Mexican immigrants, a Chicano Los Angeles poet, educator, and interdisciplinary artist. vega is the author of *zirconium ash* (What Books Press). He holds a BA from UCLA in English and an MFA in Creative Writing from CalArts. vega's poems have appeared or are forthcoming in *Diode, Dunce*

Codex, Maintenant, and elsewhere. vega is currently the Interim Executive Director of Beyond Baroque Literary/Arts Center. More @jimmyyvega or jimmy-vega.com

L.A. native, **Pam Ward** released her poetry anthology, *Between Good Men & No Man at All* (World Stage Press) in 2022 and is the author of two novels, *Want Some Get Some* and *Bad Girls Burn Slow* (Kensington). Pam's a UCLA graduate, California Arts Council Fellow, Pushcart Poetry Nominee and is a founding member of the Leimert Park Book Fair. She recently completed her novel *I'll Get You My Pretty*, featuring her aunt's role in the Black Dahlia murder.

Los Angeles poet **Dig Wayne** teaches Method Acting at the Lee Strasberg Theatre and Film Institute in West Hollywood. Originally from Ohio, Dig has lived, worked, and practiced his art in New York City and London. He has published two books of poetry, *Hip Pockets* and *Bongo Skin*. His recent collection, *One Fell Swoop* was published by innateDIVINITYbooks. His poetry has been featured in a number of literary magazines and anthologies including the last two issues of *The Sparring Artists: Anthology of Sparring with Beatnik Ghosts*.

Hilda Weiss is the co-founder and curator for www.Poetry.LA, a website that features videos of poets and poetry venues in Southern California. Her poetry has been nominated for a Pushcart prize and is published in several anthologies as well as in journals such as *Rattle, Cultural Daily, Poet Lore, Salamander,* and *Spillway* among others. Her chapbook, *Optimism About Trees*, was published in 2011. She is a fourth generation Californian and lived for many years in Topanga where she evacuated from several fires.

Jessica M. Wilson, MFA, is an International Chicana Poet, born in East Los Angeles, CA. A 3rd generation Beatnik. She's the Founder of the LA Poet Society, a poetry teacher for Cal Poets and UCLA Extension Writers Program. Jessica is an Artivist, a social justice publisher, and a DJ for Radio Ollin, KROJ 101.5 FM. Her book, *Serious Longing* was published in Paris, France. She is a mother of two and lover of 1.

Gail Wronsky, recipient of an Artists Fellowship from the California Arts Council, is the author of eight books of poetry, three coauthored collections of experimental poetry, and two books of translations of the poetry of Argentinean poet Alicia Partnoy. Newest titles include *Mockingbird's Proverbs; Born in a Barn on Venus*, with artwork by renowned artist Gronk; *Some Disenfranchised Evening*, winner of the Swan Scythe Chapbook Prize, and *Under the Capsized Boat We Fly: New & Selected Poems*. She teaches creative writing at the Catholic Workers soup kitchen in downtown Los Angeles.

Z lives in California.

www.ingramcontent.com/pod-product-compliance
Lightning Source LLC
Chambersburg PA
CBHW060452080526
44584CB00015B/1409